ORIGINAL PERFECTION

Original Perfection

VAIROTSANA'S FIVE EARLY TRANSMISSIONS

Translation and Commentary by
Keith Dowman

Foreword by
Bhakha Tulku Pema Rigdzin

WISDOM PUBLICATIONS • BOSTON

Wisdom Publications
199 Elm Street
Somerville, MA 02144 USA
www.wisdompubs.org

A previous edition of this book was published by Vajra Publications, Kathmandu, Nepal, in 2006 under the title *Eye of the Storm*.

Library of Congress Cataloging-in-Publication Data

Vairocana, 8th cent.
 [Eye of the storm]
 Original Perfection : Vairotsana's Five Early Transmissions / Translation and Commentary by Keith Dowman ; Foreword by Bhakha Tulku Pema Rigdzin.
   pages cm
 A previous edition of this book was published by Vajra Publications, Kathmandu, Nepal, in 2006 under the title Eye of the Storm.
 Includes bibliographical references and index.
 ISBN 0-86171-680-9 (pbk. : alk. paper)
 1. Rdzogs-chen. I. Dowman, Keith, translator, writer of added commentary. II. Title.
 BQ7662.4.V35 2013
 294.3'420423—dc23

                              2012049881

ISBN 9780861716807   eBook ISBN 9781614291350

17 16 15 14 13   5 4 3 2 1

Cover design by Phil Pascuzzo. Interior design by Gopa & Ted2, Inc.
Set in Garamond Premier Pro 11/14.

To the masters of the great perfection, known and unknown,
whoever they are, wherever they may be, however they appear.

Contents

ॐ

FOREWORD

THE FIVE TEXTS translated into English in this book are considered the first transmission of Dzogchen Ati to Tibet. They were transmitted by a Tibetan monk called Vairotsana who distinguished himself not only in the field of translation, emerging as the greatest of the Tibetan lotsawas, but also as a traveler and pilgrim who left the Land of the Snows for the hills of the Hindu Kush to bring back a canon of Dzogchen texts from its closely guarded source. Returning from Oddiyana, where he had received the transmission of Dzogchen Ati from Shri Singha, he immediately translated these five tantras into Tibetan, and they became known as the Five Early Transmissions or Translations (*snga 'gyur nga*). They constitute the root and essence of Dzogchen in Tibet—basic, raw Dzogchen precepts that are appropriately designated "radical Dzogchen."

Tulkus in the Nyingma tradition, considered emanations of the heart of reality, have been trained in the rites and devotions of the lineage, in the meditations and yogas of the Vajrayana, in the Buddhist philosophy of India and Tibet, and in the skillful means of assisting others not only on the path of liberation but in the amelioration of their suffering in samsara. But what precedes all of that in significance and priority, what gives it value and meaning and what facilitates the sharing of Buddhadharma, is Dzogchen Ati. This is the special, extraordinary teaching of our Nyingma lineage. The great masters, including Vairotsana, Padma Sambhava, and Vimalamitra, have all attained realization through Dzogchen, contemporary masters all owe their status to Dzogchen, and any attainment in the future will be based on the precepts of Dzogchen Ati. And while there are a vast number of texts revealing the various precepts of Dzogchen—in the Mind, Matrix and Secret Precept Series, the Elaborate, Simplified, Simple and Ultra-simple Cycles, the Crown Pith and Ultra Pith Teaching—these five transmissions of Vairotsana, the core of the Mind Series, constitute the seed, root, and branch of Dzogchen. Please remember after all, Garab Dorje himself, the first guru of the Dzogchen lineage, recited extemporaneously the greatest of these five early transmissions, *The Eternal Victory Banner* also known as *The Vast Space of Vajrasattva*, in his infancy.

If the Tibetan Dharma is to thrive in the West, it must be with the transmission of Dzogchen Ati, the apex path, the culmination of Vajrayana Buddhism, or a nondual equivalent. Throughout history, Dzogchen has been the subject of dispute among the various schools of philosophy in Tibet, but it is acclaimed by all yogins on the actual path of praxis. It is well known that it is among the personal secret practices of H. H. the Dalai Lama himself. In its transmission to the Western world, the methods of conveyance may undergo certain changes, but the essence of Dzogchen will remain unchanging. This was the teaching of our lamas Dudjom Rimpoche and Kanjur Rimpoche in their Dzogchen mandala in Darjeeling in India where I first encountered Keith Dowman, the eminent translator of these texts.

I hope many people will read these texts and realize the heart meaning and spontaneously attain the realization of Dzogchen Ati and join those who have realized this ultimate truth but remain anonymous. May all sentient beings be free from samsara!

Bhakha Tulku Pema Rigdzin
Vairotsana Foundation
Los Angeles, California
www.vairotsana.org

—————— ཨ ——————

PREFACE TO THE AMERICAN EDITION

A FTER THE PASSING of the years since this work was published in
Kathmandu, I am still satisfied with the introduction, which provides
a broad introduction to Dzogchen and particularly to the radical Dzogchen
that is found in the original transmissions that Vairotsana conveyed to the
Tibetans in the eighth century. I found myself less satisfied, however, with
the translations themselves. Vairotsana translated the original verses in a
highly ambiguous poetic style that, while transmitting a powerful blast
of radical Dzogchen, fell short of the didactic precision that would give
a translator the grammatical clues to provision of a sure interpretation.
Thus I felt that sometimes I could have been more precise in my rendering of poetic phrases—which I have taken the opportunity of this new
edition to remedy. But what about the canonical commentaries? Surely
they elucidate an unequivocal discursive meaning? Alas, the *Ten Sutras*
was written centuries later when Dzogchen was already becoming part and
parcel of a self-interested establishment and the commentaries were serving
that end. Returning to the *Ten Sutras* commentary after these intervening
years, it seems to read like a tool to assimilate the immediacy of Dzogchen's
pathless path into the spatial-temporal graduated path of Vajrayana. On
the other hand, it shows how radical an effect Dzogchen has in Vajrayana
and how it may be considered inseparable from it. From this we may infer,
indeed, that any cultural form whatsoever (Buddhist, shaman, humanist,
or post-modernist) is likewise illuminated—and released—by the light of
Dzogchen.

So in the editing of the text for this new edition, I have firstly tight-
ened the meaning by using the terminology that I have developed in the
interim. "Gnosis" (*rig pa*) is now "pure presence," for example; "equality"

is "sameness"; and "process" (path) is sometimes "modality." "Field of reality," which was used as the equivalent of *dharmadhatu*, is now "the spaciousness that is the field of reality" or an adaptation of those words. The transliteration of the Tibetan phonetic "Bairotsana" has been replaced by the more eaily recognisable Vairotsana. The appendix "Mind Series Terminology" illuminates these changes. I recommend that the reader spend some time with this appendix before entering the text to get a feel for the way many well-known Buddhist terms—such as *buddha, bodhichitta,* and *tathagatagarbha*—have been treated in the present work. Secondly, I have tweaked the verses, strengthening their radical sense while heightening the distinction between them and the commentary. In the process I have corrected some errors that had crept in during the final stages of the publication of the previous edition.

Additional material relating to *Original Perfection* can be found at www.keithdowman.net/dzogchen/eyeofthestorm.htm.

ༀ

Translator's Introduction

T HE NATURE OF Dzogchen, the Great Perfection, is perhaps best understood as the essence of all nondual mystical aspiration. Within the Tibetan context, it lies at the heart of shamanism, Bon, and Buddhism. Taking its cultural and linguistic references from Bon and Buddhism, it may appear to be limited to those traditions, but to see its existential reality restricted to that cultural frame would contradict the Tibetan precepts that define it as utterly nonspecific and unconfined. Historically Buddhism provided the ground in which the precepts of the Great Perfection appeared, and certainly it still provides a rich and wonderful metaphysical field of reference. But the principles of radical Dzogchen are appropriate to every religious and cultural context. All religion and culture is transcended by its formless essence. It subsumes science and humanism today as it once incorporated shamanism and theism. It supersedes religion by shunning dogma and doctrine. It surpasses yoga and meditation by disavowing technique. It transcends the creativity of the human mind—whether as science or art—through identity with our intrinsic nature. Inclusivity defines the Great Perfection.

As mystical endeavor the quest for natural perfection may have continued for as long as human history. Surely it is hidden in the mysteries of Babylon and Egypt, Greece and Rome, in Indian tantra, the Chinese Tao, Muslim Sufism, and in the Jewish Torah and the Christian heresies of the Albigensians, the Knights Templar, and the Alchemists, if only because natural perfection is inherent in human being and cannot be suppressed. Deprived of a lineal tradition, guides, and precepts, it may burst out spontaneously as an imperative of the human spirit, as it did in Europe and America in the 1960s. Regardless of the cultural and religious context, the time and the place, the "pathless path" of nondual illumination is always the same because the nature of the mind, being the origin of time and space, is one. It has happened, however, that in the twenty-first century the exemplars and custodians of this living tradition are the Vajrayana Buddhists of the Tibetan plateau. Nondual mysticism finds its own ground everywhere in the scope of Tibetan Buddhism, particularly in the Kagyu Mahamudra tradition, but it is in its earliest transmission into Tibet, when the tradition of the Ancients (Nyingmapa) was still in its incipient phase, that we find the most pure and unequivocal statement of the principles and poetic effusion of the heart meaning of the Great Perfection. That is what is termed "radical Dzogchen."

Given that the oldest and earliest is not necessarily the best, nevertheless, the quality of pristine freshness reverberates down the centuries from a culture on the verge of breakthrough. This quality may be discerned in eighth-century Tibet and particularly in the work of the mystic and poet Vairotsana of Pagor, who at that time wrote down the five poems presented in this book. In his work there is a sense of the light of dawn spreading over the landscape to illuminate the darkness. The word of Dzogchen had arrived to illuminate the murk of spiritualistic shamanism, to clarify the Buddhist options presented by India, China, Khotan, Brusha, and Oddiyana, and to exalt the lifestyles of the people of the Tibetan plateau. The freshness and vitality of Vairotsana's vision, written down when the Tibetan language was as young as English when Shakespeare wrote, still has the power to illuminate, although the shadows that are dispersed today are cast by apocalyptic materialism and consumerism.

The power of Vairotsana's five original works may lie in the magic of "transmission"—for that is how these poems are designated. Vairotsana did not attribute them to himself as the poet but cast them in the mold of revelations of Garab Dorje, the human source of the Dzogchen tradition, because all tantras, transmissions, and precepts of Dzogchen are said to have the same timeless origin. The verses of each of the five transmissions— consisting generally of a quatrain of two slokas, or couplets—can stand apart as didactic gems of Dzogchen expression, sometimes with only tangential connection between them, but they are better viewed as the facets of a crystal globe, each reflecting an aspect of the whole. The content of the transmissions is always the same—a unitary vision of the nature of mind. The nature of mind (where "nature" can only mean "essence") is luminous mind, the one indivisible nondual mind of natural perfection. The holistic product may be personified as the all-good buddha Samantabhadra, who at the same time is the supreme source of the transmission and the transmission itself. The reader, the recipient of the transmision, is identified, thereby, with the all-good Dzogchen vision of the transmission.

The purpose of these five poems, then, is to induce a vision of natural perfection in the mind of the reader. This is not done by logic or causal connection but through the magic, the ambiguity, of poetry. As Patrul Rimpoche writes, "We do not agree with the common dogma of traditionalists, that the only valid knowledge is mental knowledge tested by reason against textual and logical proof. Experiential understanding of the naked direct perception in primal awareness itself is the Dzogchen vision."[1] In this sense, each of the five poems constitutes a direct introduction—if not initiation— into the nature of mind and the great perfection. The experience of the transmissions themselves is self-validating, and any rational evaluation of their logic or terms of reference diminishes or blights them. The sole requisite for attaining the vision set down by the poet is a wide-open mind, and since all human beings are endowed with this mind, the great perfection is available to everyone.

The vision that these transmissions induce is not like a tantric mandala of buddhas or buddha-deities or patterned light-forms. There is not the slightest hint of symbolism, abstract or anthropomorphic. There is nothing to be seen that has any cultural specificity. There is no articulated abstruse metaphysical infrastructure to the vision. There is nothing that is not intrinsic to the nature of ordinary consciousness and the common light of day. In fact there is no trace of anything there at all. There is no structure to the vision whatsoever—the nature of the transmission is ultimately deconstructive. "Simplicity" is the one single word that may describe it. It is a holistic vision in the sense that it is all-inclusive and nondual. It consists of direct, naked perception of the nature of mind in every instant of experience.

The essence of the transmission is simple, direct perception. In the timeless moment of the here and now, there is no space for projection and filtration and no time for evaluation, reflection, and judgment. In this lies natural perfection. Herein lies the secret of nondual reality. When we speak of nondual mysticism, what is indicated is nothing but the clear light intrinsic to everyday perception; yet this perception and this function of awareness bring ultimate resolution to the human condition. All its dichotomies and contradictions are resolved in the unitary light of awareness in itself. If it can be said that conception and action exist, surely there is no gap between the initiation of the act and its actualization. The unitary moment is its own reward. Time and space are resolved in the all-inclusive wholeness of the moment. The quandaries of embodiment are resolved in each moment. The paradox and antinomies of gender are resolved in the unity of the moment. This is transmission of the Great Perfection that does not impose a new, conditional structure upon the mind but reveals what is already, primordially present. It comes by way of confirmation, then, of what has always been known: that the nature of being, the nature of reality, and the nature of mind are immanent as consummate perfection.

There is nothing in this transmission that can be grasped or conceptualized or cultivated or practiced. To assimilate it into the logical intellect and spin it out as a philosophy or doctrine is to nullify its purpose, just as the magic of poetry is lost in analysis. The transmission itself is a timeless event, like every moment of experience, arising as spontaneity, without cause or condition, so it cannot be developed into a yoga or a meditation practice. It cannot be turned into religion: there are no tenets of belief; neither devotion nor faith is a condition of its revelation; and no ritual interprets and structures it. It is simply an existential understanding of the here and now.

Vairotsana's five transmissions are compositions of deconstructive precept, expressing the Dzogchen vision of the nature of mind. Their primal impact upon a receptive reader may open a door into the vision of the great perfection. The rational mind, however, may concoct objections to such an unreferenced state and its attendant sense of identity loss. It is here that the commentary engages, providing elaboration through causal connection, lulling the intellect with its bromide, while undermining— deconstructing—the structure of the intellect by indicating the natural state of being, the suprarational reality of the great perfection that always lies immanent in the timeless moment. Here, the self-referential language of the tradition points at the unstructured ground of all language, and since this reality lies in an absence of any characteristic, attribute, or function, the Upanishadic method of "not this!" "not that!" is employed. The mystery of the Great Perfection resides in its ineffable nondual reality that is a unity but at the same time a multiplicity. It is at once the source and the creation. It is inconceivable and inexpressible. It is enlightened mind or luminous mind. To reveal all experience as this reality is the purpose of Dzogchen, and the self-evident principles of the Dzogchen Mind Series (see appendix 2) are the transmission.

There is nothing to do! "Nonaction"—or "undirected action" or "nondeliberate action"—defines the nature, ethos, and dynamic of the Great Perfection. The here and now is a field of immanent sameness, and any attempt to affect it or change it by any technique is counterproductive. Any engagement of effort diminishes it. Seeking it inhibits its discovery. Nonaction is the precept that defines the natural inclination, or lack of any inclination, of the nature of mind in order that the manifest dynamic of the field of reality is uncrystallized in pure presence.

No meditation! No discipline! The luminous mind that is the nature of all experience never comes into being or ceases to be; it cannot be created or destroyed: it has no structure. It cannot, therefore, be accessed through the structured activity of calculated discipline, and all goal-oriented meditation is such structured activity. Letting go of all practice whatsoever, including all the meditation techniques that condition the mind by focusing on an object of sight, sound, or thought, there is no meditation and only an endless continuum of luminous mind. The modality of nonmeditation and no-structure is illustrated particularly in the fourth transmission, *Pure Golden Ore*.

No progress! No development in a graduated process! The moment is perfect and complete in itself, and nothing superior can be effectuated. There is no possibility of attaining anything more desirable than the present moment. No personal growth is possible. Evolution toward a higher goal is precluded. There is no maturity to anticipate. The notion of process itself is redundant because it functions through time in a delusive linear pattern constructed by the intellect.

No place to go! The here and now is always complete in the present moment, so there is no path to follow, no quest, no journey to pursue, and no destination. It is impossible to move toward or away from luminous-mind reality, since it is always here and now. The inescapable, universal, and all-pervasive reality-modality is ever immanent. There is no destination other than the naturally liberating dynamic of the moment. This is taught particularly in the second transmission, *Radical Creativity*.

No discrimination! No prejudice or bias! The pristine awareness that is the mind's cognitive nature is utterly free of any judgmental inclination. It does not discriminate between what is good or bad, right or wrong. "Good" and "bad" are fictive labels projected upon a neutral screen that in itself is incapable of bias. Whatsoever occurs in everyday experience, excluding nothing, is suffused by this primal awareness and, moment by moment, dissolves into it. All is perfect as it stands, so nothing is rejected or avoided and nothing is accepted or favored above anything else. Nothing is embraced or appropriated and nothing spurned or suppressed. All things are always all good, and activity is always undiscriminating. This is taught in the first transmission, *The Cuckoo's Song*.

No one and no thing to change! The elements of experience, inner and outer, are part of a reality field (basic spaciousness) in which no indivisible particle can be isolated either in the laboratories of science or those of the mind. The natural unified field is a nondual reality. Every moment of experience is an ineffable expression of that field, and insofar as it is recognized as a field of cognitive being, it is known as utterly perfect and complete in itself. It cannot be improved one iota. It cannot be changed or transformed into something other than pure awareness. Because our identity—nonidentity—lies in luminous mind, whatever illusion of personality arises is utterly pristine.

No controller! No control! The control functions of the ego self-articulated in the rational mind are involuntarily superseded by the pristine awareness of the natural state of being. What appears to rise and fall as sequential instants of experience is insubstantial gossamer illusion, and the dynamic of each perfect moment is spontaneity. Any belief in a substantial, material reality, or in a "self," a "soul," an "ens," or an "atman," is delusory. There is no controller on any level and so no control. The putative controlling intellect is superseded by the intrinsic dynamic of nonaction. The here and now is free-form display, perfect in its every permutation.

The consummation of these precepts and the transmissions themselves are predicated upon an intuitive realization of the nature of mind as intrinsically pure, an assumption that is authenticated, yet neither attested nor proven, in initiatory experience. "Luminous mind" is a rendering of the Buddhist word *bodhichitta*. In Mahayana Buddhism the discursive meaning of this word is suffused by the selfless compassionate ethic of the bodhisattva intent upon giving whatsoever is required to whomsoever is in need. More technically, it is translated as "the thought of enlightenment." In Vajrayana Buddhism, where buddha-imminence is assumed, it is translated as "enlightened mind" or "awakened mind." In the Dzogchen Mind Series, this enlightened mind is the ground of all, all and everything, and the starting point, the process, and the product in one. It subsumes the field of reality, the process of release, the nature of mind, and primal awareness. Luminous mind is the nondual natural state, and so it cannot possess any definable quality, but in its vastness and depth, in its ineffable greatness, it exalts our natural state. Its primary endowment lies in direct and immediate enlightenment.

Luminous mind is personified as Samantabhadra, all-good primordial buddha—not a buddha to worship but the actuality of every moment. Those he "teaches," or manifests, are buddha and every sentient beings upon the wheel of life is free of transmigration and rebirth. His "teaching," or manifestation, is the expression of our every moment of experience in a vision of reality as the matrix of all things and all things in themselves as one. The time of his teaching is the one clear timeless moment of past, present, and future rolled into one. And the place of his teaching is zero-dimensional basic spaciousness.

In our state of natural perfection, the seemingly material world is consumed in its intrinsic nature as light by the pristine awareness inherent in every sensory perception. The four great elements—earth, water, fire, and air—that are a condensation of their spatial essence constitute basic spaciousness itself, and the luminous mind, wherein the delusive subjective and objective aspects of experience are unified, endows basic spaciousness with its own luminous display that never crystallizes as this or that. The subjective aspect of the unitary field, the sense of personal identity, is defined as the space where nothing can be found by seeking, nothing can be accomplished by endeavor, nothing whatsoever can be improved upon, and where there can be no progress or maturation. This is the natural state of primordial, preexistent enlightenment. But because that state cannot become an object of focus, since it is in no way conceivable or imaginable, determinable or demonstrable, it is better termed "nonenlightenment." Only in that sense is there universal enlightenment.

The expression of luminous mind is the compassion that suffuses our experience like water in milk. Such compassion is the potential of every possible convention and variation of human character and personality, every quality and attribute, every affectation and every foible, every vice and virtue, and every weirdness and extreme manifestation of being on the wheel of life. The psychological diversity of experience therein is expressed in the equivocal terms of men, gods, titans, hungry ghosts, animals, and hell beings. Yet the wheel of life is the expression of the compassion of luminous mind, and compassion is the wheel of life. The primordial buddha Samantabhadra embraces the totality of luminous mind as its essential emptiness, its radiant luminosity, and its compassionate expression.

The vast spaciousness of luminous mind is personified as Vajrasattva, and primal awareness is his exaltation. The spaciousness of reality is spontaneously cognitive in a nondual modality, and Vajrasattva represents the individuation of that event. That moment is inherently liberating, so there can never be any experience whatsoever that is not spontaneously and momentarily released. Vajrasattva's ineluctable presence provides that assurance. Primal awareness of the field of reality is a constant, and therefore Vajrasattva receives his name Immutable Being. The vajra is a symbol of his immovable and imperturbable nature of constant luminous awareness. His immutable dynamic is the freedom of the Great Perfection.

Insofar as there is only luminous mind in our experience, insofar as the vajra is inherent in every moment, there can never be either separation or nonseparation from Vajrasattva, which is a manner of stating the ineffable immanence of the natural state of being in the Great Perfection. So there can never be any obstacle to that natural state. What appears to obstruct the recognition of intrinsic cognitive spaciousness is attachment to the mere shimmering of gossamer phantasm, which is like a film of tarnish on pure gold. If this attachment appears to veil the nature of mind, then what is required is a fortuitous lurch into an intuition of the attachment itself as pristine awareness—a flash of realization or a recollection of initiatory experience. If the problems that arise from the exigencies of personal karma extrude into the forefront of our minds and a sense of constant interruption of the natural flow obsesses us, then what fortuitously arises is intuition of the intrinsic clarity of the glitch itself. Thus the apparent obstacles that arise in the mind provide the key to their own resolution.

Some people are convinced that their desire, anger, and emotional confusion are a thick veil over their enlightened mind, but the recognition of the light and pure pleasure in the marvelous display of energetic expression dissipates such delusive beliefs. Some are convinced that the implacable logic of the intellect and attachment to its pleasures create the trap that locks in the spaciousness, but each intellectual construct and each train of thought constitutes a door into Vajrasattva's vast space. To overcome what appear to be emotional and intellectual obstacles, people commit themselves to disciplines of lifestyle and morality, yoga and meditation, setting themselves the goal of freedom from attachment and rebirth, but the anxiety entailed by prostituting the moment for some future benefit and striving for a conceptual goal is resolved naturally in the relaxation of nonaction. The disease of calculated endeavor and goal orientation that is spiritual materialism is healed by the spontaneous and ineluctable intuition of the pure nature of mind.

The futility of trying to catch what is already in the cage or to grope all around for spectacles that are already sitting upon the end of one's nose inevitably dawns upon the goal-obsessed yogi or yogini, and it is well that we are prepared for that disillusionment by recollection of the spaciousness and radiance that we know from fortuitous initiation into the nature of mind. Decisively, we arrive at the place where the moral imperatives instilled by the plain logic and symmetry of belief in karmic concatenation are seen to provide still more of the same anxious transmigration from one neurotic trap to another and where relaxation into the timeless moment of the here and now—doing nothing—allows the clarity and emptiness of the natural state of being to shine through. When the compulsions of karmic causality and belief in moral imperatives fall away and dissolve and we surrender to the buddha dynamic of spontaneous contemplation, pristine awareness naturally prevails, superseding any residual trust in the world of karma.

With recognition of the reality thus defined, there is simultaneous recognition of the samaya commitments of Dzogchen—absence, openness, spontaneity, and unity. By their very nature, these samayas cannot be guarded or sustained. On the contrary, awareness of their actuality is a constant and natural presence that can never be vouchsafed or gainsaid. These samayas are not provisional commitments to be renounced upon reaching any goal. They are the reality of buddha here and now that can be expressed as one single commitment—commitment to pristine awareness itself. This awareness always has primacy. It is coextensive and coterminus with the space of sameness that exalts all cognition as pure presence. Pure presence is the direct experience of the moment in which there is no subjective or objective component, although in it the delusive and the nondelusive are inextricably mixed. It is intrinsic awareness of being effervescent in the timeless wholeness of purity and impurity. It is the common light of day.

What constitutes the display of Samantabhadra may not differ in kind from the forms of the neurotic universes that are being neutralized. The retinue of Samantabhadra is composed of buddha as sentient beings, and the diaphanous radiance of rainbow light suffuses the very illusions that once seemed so concrete and cloying. The projections of the psychological environments of hungry ghosts, for example, may still be in place, but now the hair-raising figments of imagination that populate those environments are like the ferocious yet empty masks of lama dance. Further, in the human realm, many people, particularly Buddhists, have entered the various graduated paths to enlightenment. Each rests on his own level, which is complete and perfect in itself. All the activities of gods and men are complete and perfect in themselves, and although they may pursue goal-oriented activity and constantly create or encounter seeming glitches in the universal process of awakened reality, the liberating capacity of Vajrasattva, who suffuses the five elements that constitute embodiment in an apparent concrete environment, is always immanent.

The different lifestyles and the associated visions, therapies, and meditation techniques employed by monks and nuns, laymen and laywomen, yogis and yoginis, and tulkus and dakinis, may be conceived of hierarchically in a pyramid of increasingly destructured mind. This ninefold hierarchy is employed by the commentary on the root verses of the texts as an index of different mind states and allows a focus upon the varying progressive approaches that, although delusive as paths to nondual reality, are perfect in themselves. Nine is a perfect or infinite number in shamanic numerology, so that the nine conventional approaches or levels that provide the mainstay subsume all others. By the same token, the nine levels of discursive meaning in the transmission, each directed toward and heard by those for whom it is relevant, subsume all other levels in the quest for the nature of mind. Further, as the traditional metaphor has it, just as a king never leaves his palace without his entourage in appropriate association, so Dzogchen Ati is always accompanied by a retinue composed of the innumerable disciplines that seek to modify or improve the human condition—for a mark of human birth is the impulsion to attain happiness. The teacher of the Great Perfection, Samantabhadra, incorporates a vast, all-inclusive retinue of beings, each preoccupied by his personal path on which appropriate transmission may be fortuitously received.

The nine approaches or levels from the apex are atiyoga, anuyoga, mahayoga, tantra- or sattvayoga, ubhayayoga, kriyayoga, and the varying praxis of bodhisattvas, hermits (pratyekabuddhas), and disciples (shravakas). On the level of atiyoga, the hyperyogin is adept in the recognition of all experience as transmission of the great perfection. On the level of anuyoga, identity of reality and pure presence, space, and awareness is shown, so that every mind-created phenomenon becomes primal awareness. On the mahayoga level, the elements of the psycho-organism and the elements of perception and the sense fields are revealed as our timeless enlightened identity; mahayoga is taught so that the structure of the conditioned mind is recognized as fivefold buddha. In the mind-created vision of tantrayoga, although the passions are not abandoned, attachment to them is utterly forsaken, and sacred substances are literally enjoyed; thereby, in signless, open vulnerability, primal awareness is facilitated and the four consorts are recognized. In ubhayayoga the identity of clear light with its colored diffusion, between self-sprung awareness and the sensory phantasmagoria, is taught. In the praxis of disciples engaged in listening and learning, hermits in ascetic retreat, and bodhisattvas in pursuit of loving-kindness, the nature of mind involuntarily shines through.

Finally, to distinguish between the recipients of these transmissions, there are those who are ready vessels with an innate affinity for the natural great perfection. This type attains the vision merely by reading the transmission or by hearing the precepts—thus "liberation by hearing." Through recognition of the natural state of mind, whatever arises is released and dissolves immediately, leaving no trace. The Dzogchen yogin or yogini's existential modality is then commensurate with the imprint of a bird in the sky. All experience is like a dance and like the free play of sensual pleasure. There is no meditation and no meditator. If glitches arise they are immediately turned into a timeless moment of mental effort and become a door back into the space of the great perfection that actually can never be relinquished. He or she assimilates the affirmation and confirmation of initiatory experience that atiyoga provides in the transmission and is absorbed without reflection in the nondiscriminatory totality of an anonymous body of light.

Then there are those who see the vision of Samantabhadra clearly through this transmission but lose it thereafter. Through a verbal introduction, or some initiatory experience, they accept the vision as the apotheosis of human nature, and with subsequent intimation of the nature of mind they enjoy nonmeditation. But then immersed in the mundane concerns of life—profit and loss, love and hate, success and failure, fame and disgrace—they see the figments of their minds as personality isolates interacting in a concrete environment, and becoming attached to seemingly external phenomena the vision of Samantabhadra is lost. Fortuitously and inevitably, however, the vision and nonmeditation does return to mind, like the rising sun, and with increased familiarity and intimacy allows fearless, wholehearted surrender to the nature of mind. Pristine awareness then resumes its natural primacy. Confidence in nonaction is reaffirmed. Belief in mental constructs slackens. Fictive projections fade away. Through the temerity of recognition of the supreme source in whatever arises, in the bardo, natural perfection is recognized in a body of light.

Then there are those who perceive the vision as through a glass darkly and, overruled by judgmental thought while reading or hearing the transmission, conceptualize it and analyze it and become susceptible to doubt. In a rationalistic process the vision is externalized and distanced and becomes a subtle and substantial goal to be achieved with a coincident sense of separation and inadequacy in the face of it. Samsara is divorced from nirvana in this process of linear thought through time, and caught on the horns of conflicting emotion we are susceptible to expectation and apprehension. "Our actions are determined by karma," we say. "We are subject to karmic retribution. We are bound to the inevitable cycle of transmigration on the wheel of time." "We have received Samantabhadra's transmission and it has given us a glimpse of perfection for a moment. But we are left with only an intellectual understanding, and it has not affected our way of being." "We live in a world of preferences and partiality, attachments and aversions, discrimination and judgment, hopes and fears." "We are not ready," we demur with a sense of our own inadequacy. "We are just beginners. We need to improve ourselves, to be good and virtuous, to control our energy patterns, to set goals and attain them, to climb the ladder of spiritual purity." Riddled by such intellectual and emotional conflict, infected by hopes and fears, we conclude that something must be done, that remedial action is prescribed in order to attain the nondual state of the vision. Such readers may go on to devote their lives to a graduated path of endeavor, practicing some meditation technique or yoga, failing to adopt recognition of the perfection of their natural state.

On the other hand, many hear the transmission and think about it, and lacking any initiatory experience they reject it and turn away. For them there never can be anything but the natural state of perfection, yet they live as beggars on the wheel of transmigration, believing that the material world is concrete and the states of mind in which they find themselves are real. Attached to the pleasant and averse to the painful, unknowingly they await the revelation of the nature of mind. So it is said.

Pagor Vairotsana: The Great Translator

In the vision of the Great Perfection, the five transmissions are Dharmakaya Samantabhadra himself. Through the medium of Vajrasattva, and the uniting of vowels and consonants, the transmission arises as a timeless display of compassionate emanation in the nature of mind. This revelation is known as Vajra Delight, or Garab Dorje, who is also the adiguru, the first nirmanakaya teacher, of the Dzogchen lineage. Pagor Vairotsana was his Tibetan translator.

In the eighth century, the locus of political and cultural vigor in Central Asia still lay in Tibet. The nomads of a united Central Tibet had created a military empire that stretched from Persia to China, from Nepal to Mongolia. Their shamanic heritage, under the influence of the sophisticated cultures that were now part of their domain, was in the process of transformation. Those cultures in the main were Buddhist, although of various hues, and along with the cavalry and diplomats, the traders and artisans, traveling the Himalayan trade routes and all bound for Lhasa, were Chan monks from China, Vajrayana panditas from Bengal, Mahayana scholars from Bihar and Khotan, tantric yogis from Kashmir and the Kathmandu Valley, Hindu sadhus from South India, and Bon shamans from the old kingdom of Zhangzhung that had dominated the Tibetan plateau before the rise of the Yarlung Valley dynasty. Buddhist temples of stone had been built in this land of yak-hair tents, and although the majority of the conservative tribal nobility opposed it, the king sponsored a monastic academy directed by a Bengali abbot who ordained a small band of Tibetan monks.

Less than a day's walk up the Yarlung Tsangpo River from the site of the new monastery, in one of the fertile side valleys to the north called Nyemo, was the village of Jekhar. It was from here that the young Vairotsana was called to Buddhist ordination by the Bengali abbot Shantarakshita. Being one of the brightest and most strongly motivated of the young monks, he was chosen to focus on the study of language. Existential concerns were a constant preoccupation among a significant element of the royal court, some of whom had also received Buddhist ordination along with Vairotsana, and discussion with visiting monks from abroad was fervent and often heated. A yogi-exorcist called Padma Sambhava, who had been invited to Samye from Kathmandu, had been successful in confronting the Bon shamans, and the Buddhists were in the ascendant. This itinerant exorcist, a Buddhist tantric sadhu wandering the Himalayan valleys for years, leaving a trail of disconsolate dakini-consorts behind him, had already gained notoriety in Tibet by seducing a local princess. He was originally from a kingdom in the far west of the Himalayas called Oddiyana, the land of the dakinis. Oddiyana had become associated with an extraordinary discipline called Dzogchen, known to the Yarlung Tibetans through their Bon confreres from Zhangzhung who had trans-Himalayan connections in Brusha and other kingdoms in the valleys of the upper Indus tributaries. Perhaps as a reaction to an overload of doctrinal dispute, perhaps based upon a natural inclination toward an effortless discipline promising immediate fulfillment, perhaps due to a secret word passed on by Padma Sambhava himself or by another itinerant yogi, a nexus of opinion formed at Samye that Dzogchen was the answer to the existential problems of the Tibetan people. Subsequently, under the auspices of King Trisong Detsen, Vairotsana and a friend were chosen to travel to Oddiyana to bring back to Tibet the Dzogchen transmission.

The direct route to Oddiyana lay up the Yarlung Tsangpo Valley, passing Mount Kailash to the south, and then continuing through the ancient Zhangzhung heartland and down the Indus Valley through Ladakh to Kashmir and Brusha and thence south to what is now Swat and eastern Afghanistan. Vairotsana's journey to Oddiyana and his meeting with the master Shri Singha is the stuff of legend. Near the Dhanakosha Lake, in a sandalwood forest, he found the old master Shri Singha, originally from the Chinese side of the Taklamakan desert, living in a nine-story pagoda. He needed first to circumvent a protective yogini-crone, a doorkeeper who barred his way, but with a totally ingenuous mind and a stash of gold coins, he passed her by and gained audience with the master. Shri Singha heard his plea for the extraordinary Dzogchen teaching and knew it was destined for the transmission to pass to Tibet. Yet he kept Vairotsana waiting until the following morning. Then he promised the young Tibetan that he would grant him the transmission on the condition that he joined the panditas studying the gradual, causal approaches during the day and only at night time receive the atiyoga teaching. Due to the Oddiyana king's jealousy of Dzogchen Ati, its propagation had been proscribed, so during the nights of transmission the master wrote down the Mind Series transmissions on white silk with goat-milk ink that would become visible only when exposed to heat. Then at Vairotsana's further urging, Shri Singha granted him the

Matrix Series precepts in the black, white, and variegated modes. Still Vairotsana was not satisfied, but Shri Singha would give him no more.[2]

After this long and intense exposure to Shri Singha, Vairotsana was finally prepared to meet the adiguru of the Dzogchen tradition, the nirmanakaya emanation of Vajrasattva, Garab Dorje himself. This apocryphal encounter occurred in a cremation ground called Dumasthira, the place of fire and smoke, and Vairotsana emerged from the meeting with the transmission of the entire 6,400,000 Dzogchen verses and a body of light.

He returned to Central Tibet by means of his newly acquired speed-walking capacity. Welcomed with all due honor, residing in the royal palace, he began a period of intense translation firstly of the five transmissions, which became known as the Five Early Translations. During this period he taught King Trisong Detsen the precepts that he was translating in the same way that Shri Singha had taught him—the progressive approach during the day and Dzogchen Ati at night. Proximity to the court, however, was to bring his honeymoon in radical Dzogchen to an end and at the same time contrive to preserve his Dzogchen lineage in Tibet during its period of greatest vulnerability. One of the king's consorts had been influenced by the long and jealous arm of the king of Oddiyana, and in order to curtail Vairotsana's teaching activity, she accused him of raping her and sought to have him banished. The king was reluctant to believe his queen, but eventually succumbing to her repeated denunciation, he exiled Vairotsana to Tsawa Rong in the country of Gyelmo Rong in Kham, in eastern Tibet. There Vairotsana taught Dzogchen to three yogins, among whom Yudra Nyingpo was the principal, establishing a separate and enduring Dzogchen tradition in the east of the country.

When the climate at court finally turned clement, Vairotsana was recalled from exile and continued to teach and translate in Central Tibet. The principal recipients of his transmission were Nyak Jnana Kumara and the Khotanese queen Liza Sherab Dronma. Later he was invited to Khotan and taught there and passed away in that foreign land. Vairotsana is part of the root of most of the Tibetan Dzogchen lineages.[3]

NOTES ON THE TEXT

The Five Early Translations are found in the Collected Tantras of Vairotsana (*Bairo rgyud 'bum*), a compendium that was compiled probably in the twelfth century. During the same period they were assimilated to the

Supreme Source (*Kun byed rgyal po*), the encyclopedic Dzogchen Mind Series tantra that took pride of place as the first text in the atiyoga section of the Collected Tantras of the Ancients (*Rnying ma rgyud 'bum*). This last collection went through various mutations and is our primary source of Dzogchen texts today (see appendix 1). The second text in the atiyoga section of the Collected Tantras of the Ancients is called the *Ten Sutras* (*Mdo bcu*), a commentary on Vairotsana's five transmissions and a rich source of Dzogchen precepts in itself. It is this text that is the source of my commentary. It was written by an unknown author, again probably in the twelfth century.

In the text herein the lines that introduce each of the transmissions are my synthesis of material taken from the *Supreme Source* and the *Ten Sutras*. The root verses are translations of the best readings I could elicit from the various sources. The commentary on the verses is my paraphrastic translation of the *Ten Sutras'* commentary with explanatory notes interpolated. *The Eternal Victory Banner: The Vast Space of Vajrasattva*, by far the longest of the transmissions, is divided into twenty-seven parts, or "timeless moments," headings found in the Collected Tantras of Vairotsana edition. The headings to the commentaries to the *Eternal Victory Banner* verses are taken from the *Ten Sutras*. The final line of the commentaries in this section is a summation of the discursive meaning of the entire verse. The annotation to the text indicates only a few of the discrepancies between the various sources.

ACKNOWLEDGMENTS

With deep gratitude and deference I thank all the masters of the Tibetan tradition who have given me transmission, in particular Dudjom Rimpoche and Kanjur Rimpoche, who were both heart sons of the great treasure-finder Trinle Jampa Jungne; also to my friend and mentor Bhakha Tulku Pema Rigdzin, a Dzogchen yogi, for all his kindness; to Chogyal Namkhai Norbu, the terton-king of our age, for his spacious understanding; to Adriano Clemente for his spadework on the texts; and to Terese Coe and Sondra Hausner for their immaculate editing.

THE CUCKOO'S SONG OF PURE PRESENCE

IN TIBET'S ancient shamanic tradition, the cuckoo was a magical bird, the king of birds. As the cuckoo's first call is the harbinger of spring, so the six lines of the *Cuckoo's Song of Pure Presence* introduce the reality of Dzogchen. In this seminal transmission, Samantabhadra defines himself as spontaneously complete and perfect nonaction. It incorporates the precept of undiscriminating joyous activity. This is the root text of the Dzogchen Mind Series.[4]

Hey, Mahasattva, Magnificent Being, listen!

The nature of multiplicity is nondual
and things in themselves are pure and simple;
being here and now is construct-free
and it shines out in all forms, always all good;
it is already perfect, so exertion is redundant
and spontaneity is ever immanent.

All experience, the entire phantasmagoria of the six senses, the diverse multiplicity of existence, in reality is without duality. Even if we examine the parts of the pure essence of mind in the laboratory of the mind, such specifics are seen to be illusive and indeterminate. There is nothing to grasp and there is no way to express it. The suchness of things, their actuality, left just as it is, is beyond thought and inconceivable, and that is the here and now. Yet diversity is manifestly apparent, and that is the undiscriminating, all-inclusive sphere of the all-good buddha, Samantabhadra. Total perfection has always been a fact, and there has never been anything to do to actuate this immaculate completion. All endeavor is redundant. What remains is spontaneity, and that is always present as our natural condition.

If the six lines are divided into three pairs of verses describing Dzogchen vision, meditation, and action respectively, the first two lines express the view that luminous mind is an ineffable singularity and cannot be analyzed; the second two lines indicate nonmeditation as the natural state of Samantabhadra's display; and the third couplet shows action as the nondirected action—nonaction—of spontaneous awareness.

--- ༄ ---

RADICAL CREATIVITY

SAMANTABHADRA'S RADICAL CREATIVITY is the miracle of illusory display emanated in every instant. It lies in the free-form field of reality, driven by the dynamic of nonaction. In a more limited sense, however, radical creativity is evident here in the soft touch of Samantabhadra's breath of inspiration that informs these pith instructions. This is a transmission that embodies specific instruction. It teaches that there is no path to traverse and no distinctions to be made in luminous-mind reality.[5]

Hey, Mahasattva, Magnificent Being, listen!

1

**All and everything emanates from me,
so all and everything, whatever appears,
is revealed as transmission,
revelation of timelessly pure basic spaciousness.**

The path is the process of unfoldment of Samantabhadra's entire emanation in a timeless moment. In this respect every moment is identical and complete in itself, and there can be no progress or development in or of luminous mind. There can be no gradual increase or decrease of realization through time. Further, if all is one in the moment, how can there be any valid differentiation of luminous mind from reality or, indeed, any distinctions whatsoever? Samantabhadra's all-inclusive momentary emanation is the nonreferential field of reality, which is his transmission and his instruction. The here and now is luminous mind, the field of reality, and Samantabhadra's complete transmission. There is nothing else.

2

**All outer and inner is the timeless field of spacious reality,
and in such an immaculate field of play,
buddha and sentient beings are not distinct—
so why try to change anything?**

Luminous mind and reality are one in basic spaciousness, and it is quite impossible to make any distinction. We say that all phenomena, whatever exists, composed of earth, water, fire, air, and space, is external and that luminous mind and the nature of reality are internal. But this is idle speculative thought imputing mere nominal meaning where there is no real basis for it. The field of reality is an all-inclusive unity. In this timeless sphere of activity there is no distinction between buddha and sentient beings. It is impossible to improve on the timeless moment—it is already perfect and complete, the all-good Samantabhadra. It cannot be altered or transformed because it is the immutable Vajrasattva.

3

**There is no ambition in effortless, fully potentiated creativity,
and such free-form spontaneous perfection is always the same;
in the pure field of reality, where the conception and the act are one,
however misguided, how can we innocents do any wrong?**

A moment of bodhi reality is primordially perfect and lacks any goal orientation or ulterior intent; it has no desire. It is free of all aspiration. It is uncontrolled and uncontrollable free-form display. Every moment of reality is the same in the ultimate sameness of luminous mind. The heart meaning is always the same. Since it is complete and perfect as it stands, there is nothing at all to do, and there never was anything to do, and thus activity is free-form display. All strenuous practice is rendered ineffective. Here, both impulse and its simultaneous actualization, and both immaculate subject and object, are the pure field of reality. In this milieu it is impossible to err, regardless of our naive beliefs and intractable habits. Nothing we fools can do can defile this pure space.

4

The pure-pleasure union of sentient behavior,
conceived by the deluded as a perverse path,
is identical to the pure modality of Samantabhadra:
whoever understands such sameness is buddha, lord of all.

Pure-pleasure union, sensory or sexual, whether as an integral part of human conduct or as a tantric path, is reviled as immoral or perverse by the ignorant. But the course of human behavior, from the beginning, is inseparable from Samantabhadra's transmission as revealed above—free-form play. These two paths are actually one. The "lord" of past, present, and future, buddha is the realization that these apparently incompatible modes are identical.

All dualities, all dualistic structures, are spontaneously resolved in the ultimate sameness of Dzogchen. This includes the duality of the delusive path of gender union and the luminous mind modality where the vision and the act are one. The apparent duality of the gender principles of skillful means and insight united in pure pleasure is actually always a unity from the beginning, a primordial unity, pulled apart (in anuyoga) only in order to recognize it as a unity and always for the first time.

5

On the delusive, extremist path, thinking, "I" and "mine,"
deluded innocents enter a structured path of Dharma practice
with no chance to realize that it leads nowhere:
How can reality ever be found by seeking?

The teacher who talks in terms of "I" and "mine" implies the existence of a substantial self—or soul—in others who therefore must strive to gain and hold something that they lack. This conventional way of thinking is called "extremist" because of its lack of a sense of middle way where the "I" is deconstructed and the notion of possession becomes a fallacy. Such a teacher draws his students into a conceptual, progressive, goal-oriented dharma practice, where there is a presumption that the graduated path has an attainable goal and that realization can be obtained through analysis and where there is no possibility of spontaneous realization. The path of ritual performance and religious practice has no end. In the great perfection there is no path—only the timeless modality of momentary unfoldment. Thus the nature of reality cannot be found by seeking; it is already present. The mind cannot objectify its own nature, so reality cannot be found by searching for it. Seeking it would be like a dog chasing its own tail.

6

The instruction of monkey-like masters who lack direct insight
is fraught with false concepts of preparation and technique;
so the master who cleans the tarnish from pure gold,
the authentic teacher, the most precious resource,
he is worth a ransom of any vast price.

Like a monkey who mimics without understanding is the teacher who gives precept and transmission without the valid basis of understanding that is direct insight into the nature of mind. Such teaching induces in the mind of the disciple a conceptual notion of the path, a specific starting point and a goal involving preparation, supports, and technique. The master who sees the nature of mind has eradicated any implication of a conditioned path. This is likened to removing any fine film of tarnish from pure gold through the application of black alum—a traditional practice. No refinement, like separating the dross from pure gold, is necessary. The teacher's transmission of this pathless path is worth to his students whatever price must be paid. In early times the student proved his commitment by offering gold to the master.

---------------------------------- ཨ ----------------------------------

The Great Garuda in Flight

THE GARUDA is a giant mythical eagle-like bird. In the mountains he glides high in the sky, wide wings outstretched, riding the currents of air, occasionally beating his wings in unison. He seems to put no effort into his flight. He is utterly alone there. He appears to be flying purely for the joy of it. He has mastery.

Samantabhadra, Luminous Mind, taught this seminal transmission on effortless perfection, undirected free-form action, so that the mind can rest at ease. It shows that there is nothing substantial in the mind, that there is no quest to pursue and no possible progress on a path toward a goal, and that reality cannot be demonstrated or proven in any way and is immune to inflating or deflating evaluating bias.

Within this uncompromising description of the great garuda in flight— the Dzogchen yogi in a nondual modality—there appear references to glitches and veils and also allusions to the keys to the doors through which the existential miasma may be forsaken.[6]

Hey, Magnificent Immutable Being, listen!

1

Hey, this free-form field, illusive like space,
nowhere located, has no object of focus;
an unstructured experiential process,
it occurs in the slightest subtle projection:
the concept of pure being, indeterminable,
itself is self-sprung awareness,
a ubiquitous, unthinking, authentic presence,
and this free-form field needs no alteration.

The field of nonaction, a free-form field of reality, is the basic spaciousness that is the dharmadhatu itself, and its pristine awareness is everywhere naturally present. The projected fields of dualistic perception are instantaneously transcended as a spontaneously emergent, nonobjective field of reality. Therein lies the timelessly unfolding modality.

Pure being, the dharmakaya, although conceived as an object in contrived meditation, has no content, no specific qualities, and no actuality, and hence the ubiquitous self-sprung awareness. Think of pure being—a thoughtless, boundless space of sameness—and the mind is filled by the nondual actuality of spontaneous pristine awareness. Luminous mind is at once the sole cause and effect, and for that reason, when relativistic thought forms arise in pure being, they are emerging spontaneously as a free-form field of pristine awareness.

The reality of nondual perception is an integrated field in which objects cannot be located or isolated as discrete entities. The innate tendency of the intellect to concretize and reify is perceived here as a subtle projection or "dedication" that is immediately recognized as the field of reality. It is as if the structuring, conceptualizing tendency of conditioned mind instantaneously unfolds into an insubstantial, unstructured, and inconceivable field of spaciousness. Thus the dualism of subjective knower and any objective factor never arises. There is only ever pure being, simultaneously a concept of emptiness and an existential reality. Any slight projection that gives intimation of a putative duality is immediately released by itself. Each thought and concept has, intrinsic, its own automatic release function: as pristine awareness it swallows itself.

Thus the natural field of reality cannot be improved upon, and there is nothing at all to be done to attain it. Indeed, there is no object to address in this field, so how can anything be done to it? Any goal-oriented meditative technique employed to discover it is a vain counterproductive attempt that seeks to turn it into an object; but the nature of the causal method itself cannot but find the reality of the pure essence of mind.

2

Seeking the essence in interdependent phenomena,
enjoy it only in its nonconceptual aspect,
for the manifest essence is just pure being.

The field of experience is perfected as it stands, and nothing needs to be done to actualize it as pure being. In whatever manner the pure essence of mind appears, the appearance itself finds its own intrinsic reality. Its seeming appearance is recognized as inconceivable, and so its manifestation is free of mental structuring and only as such, free of constructs, can it be enjoyed. "Interdependent phenomena" is to be understood as the relative world that arises through the mutual dependence of twelve causes and conditions (ignorance, habitual tendencies, consciousness, name and form, six sensory fields, contact, feeling, craving, existence, birth, old age, and death). But what appears to be interdependent phenomena is the free-form field of the pure essence of mind. "The basic spaciousness that is the field of reality, unchangeably empty, is known through reflections in the nature of mind."[7] The analysis of samsara as a twelvefold causal chain may be employed in the meditation technique whereby the emptiness of each link is established and the source of samsara revealed. But in the view disclosed here, the twelve concepts in themselves—nothing but pure being—are the means to their own immediate consummation [see also verses 24 and 25].

Relaxing into every concept with an empty mind, the pristine awareness of pure being, which is the individuated pure essence of mind, is spontaneously present. Thus the marvelous display of Samantabhadra is enjoyed as its inconceivable, unstructured nature. Since the pure essence of mind is intrinsic to all, nothing but pure being can ever arise out of it, and there is nothing else to achieve. To put it another way, the natural expression of pure being is its own antidote, and it is reflexively released into itself.

3

This all-inclusive particle, indivisible and unpatterned,[8]
is the nonspecific actuality of pristine awareness;
in that vivid, unthought, wide-open essence
on the path of purity lies sovereign sameness.

This one indivisible particle that can never be particularized or localized is the luminous mind essence evoked in the previous verse. Within it, pristine awareness, being noncomposite, arises by and from itself. The singularity of this reality is the nonspecific heart meaning that is the exaltation of pristine awareness. Pristine awareness arises spontaneously in and as the unitary significance of things. This primordial awareness of pure being suffuses all seemingly concrete phenomena in a unitary cognition. It is vivid direct perception, unthought and unstructured, an open-ended expanse. In the modality of utter purity that is immersed in this perceptual nonduality lies effortless awareness of sameness, the natural sameness of all things, and this is the nature of the pure essence of mind.

4

Changeless and unchangeable, there is nothing to desire,
no object of perception, no perceiving mind;
impulsion toward direct self-perception implies fixation on a cause,
but no ultimate sameness can come in the bliss of meditation
**   infatuation.**

This naturally arising pristine cognition precludes attachment because it has no object within it to grasp and to cling to. In the absence of any object of attachment, there is no mind to cling and no mind to grasp, and so mind is unlimited. There is only the here and now. Subjective and objective factors are resolved in unitary cognition. The unchangeable nature of that awareness is like a timeless, primordial absence of object to be grasped and grasping mind. If, nevertheless, we are still struck by the imperative to seek and find the nature of mind—that timeless primordial absolute—on a path of direct vivid pure presence, then that implies fixation on a causal path of meditation. Employing such technique, most likely we will become intoxicated and obsessed by the pleasure that arises in the projective mode of meditative absorption. In that pleasure-attachment, the possibility of attaining the famous sovereign sameness is denied.

5

In the unitary, all-embracing buddha-dimension, nothing can
**   be added,**
and since basic spaciousness is unbounded, it cannot be diminished;
in the reality display there is no place of special heightened mood,
for pleasure resides everywhere equally in the vast self-sprung field.

In this nondual perspective "the one buddha-dimension" is all-inclusive pure being (dharmakaya), which subsumes the dimensions of clarity (sambhogakaya) and compassion (nirmanakaya). From the beginning it is complete and perfect in itself, and nothing can augment or improve it.

Likewise, since the reality of self-sprung awareness cannot be reached by movement in any direction, its spaciousness that is the field of reality is the limitless here and now and cannot, therefore, be circumscribed. Thus in nondual luminous mind experience, there is no variation in mood, only the one taste of pure pleasure, for reality is the play of pleasure and the field of reality is the playground of pleasure.

6

**There is no marvelous vision to be seen here with an eye of insight
and, since nothing can be explained, nothing specific to be heard;
here the sacred and profane are always inextricably intermingled,
and an ultimate goal, a superior place, cannot be articulated.**

There is no particular understanding or insight to be desired above any other, for all cognition is equal in pure being. There is no particular way of seeing that will provide insight into the here and now, for the here and now is always present. It is useless to wait to hear something of particular significance because, in the moment, heart meaning remains unelaborated and cannot be expounded. If the "sacred," the "real," is seeming appearance and the "profane," the "unreal," is pure fabrication,[9] because verbal expression is an inextricable mixture of these two, it is impossible to articulate the ultimate reality, which is supposedly a superior state. The ultimate reality of "absolute emptiness," being expressed and defined, does not exist in reality and cannot be established existentially.

7

**The path of luminous mind cannot be conceived as true or false
because self-sprung awareness itself cannot be defined;
in the direct vivid presence of timeless inclusive identity,
thought arises but like a shadow.**

Any attempt to determine the manifest luminous mind, the appearances that flit across the mind-sky, as real or unreal, authentic or contrived, true or false, is purely academic. Such discussion is informed by mental constructs, which cannot comprehend the spontaneous nature of mind. The self-cognizing mind-sky itself surpasses its content. In the free-form identity lacking directed activity, pure presence does not seek to identify itself. In pristine awareness, constructs and discursive thoughts are like gossamer shadows without weight or substance. They are buddha shadow, and a shadow is all we can see of it. They are like rainbow-hued figments of mind, neither existent nor nonexistent, neither coming into existence nor ceasing to be.

Every verbal expression in mind or speech is transcended by its nature as the pristine awareness that occurs at one with the verbal formula. Thus the alphabetic glyphs of thought and speech—whether they express positive or negative discursive meanings—are buddha speech, and it is pointless to discuss with oneself the validity of any given experience with a view to any imagined conclusion. Attachment to any particular premise, hypothesis, or formula over any other is thereby preempted, and argument or discussion becomes a dead issue. Every experience is consummate in itself.

8

Its nonexistence is not unqualified—its essence emerges as an absence,
and its emptiness is not voidness—it is present as empty objects;
through recollection of the nature of space, without desire,
the pleasure of consummate free-form action is enjoyed,
and in that untargeted field, pristine awareness emerges.

The essence does not exist as any thing but emerges as an absence of anything else. Likewise emptiness is not voidness because it is present as an empty field. The "nonexistence" and "emptiness" of the pure essence of mind are conceptual tools that deny it substantiality and create an ineffable space in which nonaction and spontaneous creativity occur. "Absence" or "nonexistence" describes the source—the pure essence of mind—of a nonobjectifiable field or object. "Emptiness" indicates only the absence of anything concrete or specific in that field and, further, implies the infusion of such an indeterminate reality by a vital fullness. Space is its best analogue and, indeed, by evoking the experience of the nature of space, free of any desire or intention, the pure pleasure of luminous mind emerges in a free-form field suffused by pristine awareness.

9

The ancient ascetics, focusing a passionate will,
became utterly lost in the torment of strenuous effort;
the omniscience that is immersion in the natural process,
if it is articulated, engenders conceptual meditation.

Referring back to the sages of yore[10] to exemplify a nonproductive, self-defeating mode of meditation, their endeavor was doomed not so much by strenuous, passionate effort but by the construction of goals fixed by conceptualizing the undoubted state of omniscience of those who had recognized the true nature of mind. Omniscience is the quality of nonconceptual pristine awareness; when such natural understanding is defined as knowledge of this or that through metaphysical speculation and conceptual fabrication, it is turned into a desirable goal and spontaneity is precluded. The rishis pursued a futile temporal path of conceptual goal-oriented meditation.

10

Craving pure pleasure is an attachment sickness;
if it is not cured by the panacea of imperturbable sameness,
even the causal bases of higher states are infected by passion.

Desire for happiness or pleasure through meditation is as much an extraneous attachment as desire for sensual pleasure or material objects. Hunger for pure pleasure is chronic heart disease. The universal panacea for desire and attachment is our inborn imperturbable sense of the sameness of all experience. Without this natural recognition, desire nullifies even the merit accumulated for the purpose of attaining a higher state of being. Without it, social virtues such as generosity, patience, and morality are infected and skewed. So the desire that fuels the ambition to attain a spiritual goal is self-defeating.

Desire in itself is self-liberating, but with craving and addiction—like diseased attachment to the bliss of union—desire becomes a glitch in the process. It is the presence of the sameness that takes the sting out of desire and allows it spontaneous liberation. Even if it is desire for the virtue-creating states of beatitude that is infected by goal-oriented craving, the same applies.

11

Those enmeshed in a negative process by this virulent disease,
aching for progress, are like animals stalking a mirage—
their destination has no existence anywhere;
the causal bases of even the ten stages obscure the purest mind.

Goal-directed craving entails a negative process that is like pursuing a phantom—the goal is a figment of the imagination and cannot be reached no matter how long the journey. Nirvana can never be reached by striving. The principle applies equally to those seeking a mundane goal as to those who strive to traverse the ten stages of the bodhisattva path—the stages and levels cannot be traversed so long as they are separated from the starting point in the here and now, where pristine awareness is an immediate source of fulfillment. Even when the goal is one of the ten stages of purification on the bodhisattva path or buddha itself, ambition to attain it is a glitch in the natural process.[11]

12

Ultra fast pristine awareness—beyond thought,
like a spiritual friend—a fountain of gems,
unmotivated and independent of changing circumstance
by its very nature fulfills all wishes.

Goal-oriented striving is redundant because pristine awareness itself—moving so fast that fulfillment is simultaneous with the need—is totally satisfying. Such pristine awareness is like the wish-fulfilling gem of the masters that is the source of infinite virtue, the precious jewel that we carry in veneration upon our heads. It is like a soul mate who responds to our unspoken wishes, has no self-directed or ulterior motivation, and remains constant in all circumstances whatsoever. It is not something that can be imaged or is contingent upon circumstance. It is pure presence arising from within as our own nature—that is what is totally satisfying.

13

Analyzed it is nothing—letting it be, fine exaltation!
It is truly invisible, yet it gratifies every need:
the master, innocent of self and other, a treasure trove;
the Happy Isles, revealed in selfless compassion.

This precious wish-fulfilling gem of pristine awareness when examined under the microscope appears nonexistent. But naturally relaxing into it, it spontaneously emanates a multiplicity of positive qualities; it is the invisible matrix that emanates the resolution of all our needs, and here the great way is revealed to all. In pristine awareness, where the duality of subject and object, self and other, is resolved, there is the master, the guru-buddha, and the teacher. That is the land of milk and honey, where everything is fulfilled, a field of instantaneous accomplishment. The master is a bodhisattva in his pure land, which is an emanation of selfless compassion. This is the emanation body (tulku) that never leaves its luminous mind source and never becomes a concrete object, and this is the wish-fulfilling gem.

14

Unmoving within, it is nothing that can be found within,
and turning outside, it cannot be imaged or isolated;
neither extruding nor intruding, this selfless compassion
is inalienable—it abides here timelessly.

This precious jewel of selfless compassion is identical to luminous mind and, like awakened mind, it is said to exist within but cannot be discovered within or indeed anywhere at all. Certainly it cannot be found outside because what appears outside is a projection upon an empty screen and has no substantial reality whatsoever. So this selfless compassion can be neither radiated nor absorbed, neither applied to another nor soaked up from outside, for it cannot move out of its own sphere, which is all embracing. In no way can it be intentionally or conscientiously applied to an external human or material field or can it reduce itself to mawkish pity. It cannot be focused upon a specific target of sympathy. It is a primordial, universal constant.

15

To yearn for pleasure precludes its dawning—
pleasure is already here, yet still it strains for itself;
in pure delusion we ardently crave nirvana,
but such a grasping self has no buddha vision.

Incessant desire toward a future end frustrates itself because the actual process of desire in this moment is the end itself. Consummation cannot be attained until desire is recognized as the pure pleasure that it always is. The desire for pleasure that looms out of luminous mind strains toward what is always ineluctably present in the here and now as pure pleasure. In the same way, the desire for nirvana that arises in clouded pristine awareness is consummated only when it recognizes itself as nirvana. So long as it strains toward nirvana, the aspiration alienates itself from nirvana, and in such a bind the nature of the aspiration as the goal remains obscured. Rather than trying to perform the impossible task of standing aside and admiring luminous mind, we jump directly into it.

16

Where there is no buddha, there is no buddha to name,
and buddha revealed, to label it is error:
to try to catch buddha "out there" is a false path,
for all things are formless without an iota of substance.

So long as dualistic perception maintains a gap between desire and pleasure, so-called buddha cannot be seen. In the absence of buddha, to employ the concept is to suggest something that does not exist and that creates a dichotomy between what is and what might be. To strive for what might be is a chimerical, mistaken quest because buddha has no color or shape and does not exist anywhere. Buddha has no substance or continuity whatsoever, so the label does not refer to any entity or state. Then, when buddha is revealed, there can be no objectification of nondual buddha. It cannot be conceptualized and "he who knows does not speak." So the word *buddha* remains phony in any context, and whether in a delusive or nondelusive state he who speaks does not know.

17

Consummate, beyond desire, serene,
insubstantial, and utterly foregone,
the nature of the miraculous ambrosia
does not depend upon any technique.

The "miraculous ambrosia" is nondual perception where conscious subject and animate or inanimate object are indissolubly joined in the totality of pristine awareness. This ambrosia (*amrita*) is, therefore, pristine awareness itself, which is spontaneously, effortlessly, and ineluctably present in every moment. There is no need to apply any technique whatsoever to attain the release, and the shape and color of the immaterial form that is abandoned there matters not at all. The neurosis of clinging and the pain of attachment are naturally and primordially assuaged.

18

This sublime reality, free and open, all inclusive,
provides recourse for the little ones,
but when concepts dissolve in the vastness,
there is no distinction between great and small.

The antidote to the goal-oriented aspirations of adherents to the lesser—causal—levels of disciples, hermits, and bodhisattvas is the vast expanse of naturally perfected reality. In this space all ideas about the nature of reality dissolve, all desire, aspiration, and ambition dissolve, all concepts projected upon the sensory fields dissolve. There is only one recourse, technique, or antidote, and that is primordial luminous mind, which is not to be sought after.

19

Articulated transmissions, emergent visions,
like an illusionist's trick,
arise in pulsating misty awareness.

Transmission that is verbalized extempore and augmented by secret instruction, or a vision taking momentary form, is like a conjuror's magic—mere illusion. Now you see it; now you don't! It appears to have content, but it is utterly insubstantial. Such creativity arises through the power of pristine awareness pulsating in sameness, creating a skein of illusion at each beat, at each beat engulfed in its own purity. Through the self-recognition of ultimate sameness in a torpid mind, pristine awareness is freed from its seeming dullness and cloudiness.

Within seeming delusion, pristine awareness emerges spontaneously. In the very process of the volatile fluctuations of delusive energy, in its dispersion and absorption, expansion and contraction, its oscillation between creative output and ultimately deconstructive rest, pristine awareness arises in sameness. In this way, verbal transmission is the inspired revelation of a dynamic pulsating pristine awareness. Vision arises by the same process. Poetry and art arise likewise. Scripture has the same source. Out of a languid, torpid mind, primal awareness shines through and therefore can be said to be the source of spontaneous creativity. [This precept is restated in *Pure Golden Ore*, verse 5, and *Eternal Victory Banner*, verse 44.]

20

In this universal sovereign approach,
released, accepting, our nature
aspires to nothing, appropriates nothing,
and induces not the slightest presumption.

Self-sufficient, we are released from all conceptual supports and mental
crutches, free of a spiritual base or port. With presence of sameness we are
undiscriminating. We have no desires and no needs. The ingenuousness of
our pleasure assures that no complacence or arrogance can be generated,
and this frees us from the seeming womb-like security of the gods. The
universality of the process where the upper and lower realms are one, and
buddha and sentient beings are indivisible, denies the possibility of the
gods' exclusivity as also the sages' divine pride.

21

As with the soaring garuda in flight,
no complication, no simplification,
nothing to lose and nothing to gain.

The garuda, the mythological king of birds, emerges from his egg fully
mature, and at birth he can glide across the universe with a single movement of his wings. Utterly self-sufficient, fearless, lacking any anxiety, he
needs no output or input, radiates nothing and absorbs nothing, without
diffusion or focus; flying high and free he is completely happy in himself
without expectation or trepidation, hope or fear.

22

That ultimate space that is like the ocean
gives rise to the multiplicity of things;
creative potential, coextensive with space,
is unpredictable in the forms that it takes.

The ocean is the source of all variety. Still in its depths, its surface spontaneously takes on all peaceful and wrathful forms representing every kind of
human experience. Just as the shape of the ocean's surface is capricious and
variable, so the form of creation, the shape of our experience, is changeable,
variable, and unpredictable. The creativity of the pure essence of mind is

all-pervading like space, and where it appears to manifest as this or that is always uncertain.

23

In the pure essence of mind,
ultimate sovereign samadhi arises spontaneously,
and vision is like a vast ocean,
unstructured, as extensive as space.

The creative dynamic of the pure essence of mind is ubiquitous, although its point of apparent manifestation is uncertain. In every adventitious thought or construct, the ultimate samadhi always arises without concentration or relaxation. With that, then, vision is like a vast ocean or like the sky. Vision has no structure, or it is simultaneously structured and destructured. Thought-free with the sense of sameness, it is coextensive with space. That is the vision.

24

In this free-form field of Samantabhadra,
nothing is born and nothing transforms;
the twelvefold causal chain
denigrates and demeans it.

In Samantabhadra's field of activity, which is the space of sameness, nothing is born and nothing dies, nothing comes into being and nothing ceases to be; nothing can transform or transmigrate and there is nothing at all that can change. Causality is nullified, so there is no karma and no reincarnation. The twelvefold chain of interdependent origination (ignorance, habitual tendencies, consciousness, name and form, the six sensory fields, contact, feeling, craving, existence, birth, and old age and death) is an analysis of samsara, the wheel of life. Entertaining such a theory denigrates and demeans the original buddha, Samantabhadra, by imputing a causal process to what is timeless. Causality precludes the perfection of the here and now by the presumption of causes and conditions. It is the premise of an intractable pessimist. But to deny the causal chain diminishes samsara while to affirm it reifies its fleeting appearances—and neither is appropriate to recognition of its nature.

25

Let the wise recognize the twelvefold chain
as a door into delusive understanding for the ignorant;
experience of the six kinds of mythic beings
should be recognized as the primary path.

If we believe in samsara, affirming the existence of its causes and conditions, a door into samsara's six realms of suffering opens, and endless transmigration from realm to realm begins. The ignorant who walk through that door are trapped by delusive appearances. But whoever recognizes the nature of reality understands the twelve links and samsaric appearances as mere concepts and constructs. At the same time, delusory samsaric experience of the six personality types—the six kinds of mythic beings who populate the six realms of the wheel of life—recognized by the wise as luminous mind itself, constitutes the enlightened modality. In this way, what represents a trap for those who affirm or deny samsara and its causal rhetoric is a lucky break for those who understand it as a luminous-mind process.

26

Since sensual pursuits are whetted by compassion,
the pleasure of luminous mind is enacted in them all;
butchers, whores, and taboo-breakers,
unspeakable sinners and outcastes,[12]
all can know nothing but pure pleasure
through inclusive perfection, the nondual elixir.

When there is no gap between vision and action on the wheel of life, when vision and action are congruent and simultaneous, whatever form the sensory continuum takes, regardless of social opprobrium or taboo, there can only be pure pleasure. In nondual perception the apparent form is always mere gossamer illusion of luminous mind. All activity is suffused by compassion for others. This includes the activity of butchers and all erotic indulgence—all is luminous-mind action, and pure pleasure is its inevitable feeling tone. Even the breaking of social taboos is suffused by compassion, regardless of whether it is a single action or lifestyle. The five taboos, or inexpiable crimes, of the Buddhist tradition are matricide, killing an arhat, patricide, creating schism in the community, and letting the blood of a tathagata with malice—these actions are said to result in immediate rebirth in hell without a moment for absolution. The elixir of nonduality absolves—absolutely—all guilt, and in ultimate sameness there can only be pure pleasure.[13]

27

**This unstructured, unthought, pure essence of mind
cannot be hidden in the continuum of mind:
for undiscriminating luminous-mind yogis,
luminous mind is present in every situation.**

Our actual identity, being all-inclusive, perfect, and complete, our identity as luminous mind, is inseparable from pure pleasure. It is known as "the inconceivable essence." It is not something discrete concealed somewhere in the continuity of being or in the personality. It is there for everybody to see in every situation that arises. As we act without discrimination, neither rejecting nor adopting whatever arises, it is implicit in the sense of total fulfillment. Nothing lacking, nothing superfluous, it resides in the absence of motivation. It is the equanimity that exists in experience of the thing-in-itself, the essence of unstructured experience. It exists as the nature of mind in the continuity of thought.

PURE GOLDEN ORE

JUST AS ORE is suffused by pure gold so all experience is pervaded by luminous mind. The ore, indeed, is as good as gold. Experience of all things composed of the five elements is thus the pure-luminous-mind teacher. Here Samantabhadra transmits the heart meaning of that axiom. Natural nonaction is the theme, and nonmeditation is the mode. Manjushri, the gentle virgin prince, is evoked as the exemplar of this unequivocating transmission. The yogin rests naturally in the spontaneous pleasure of effortless perfection![14]

Hey, Magnificent Being, listen!

*1 Luminous Mind Is the Light of Buddha and the Heart
of All Things*
**Luminous mind, inexpressible, beyond ideation,
as the light of the teacher is extolled by all;
as the heart of experience it is the gentle prince
resting in the spontaneous pleasure of effortless perfection.**

In the pure essence of mind, a samadhi exists that transcends the entire field of ideas and is beyond expression. Resting in the samadhi that is beyond mentation, buddha is perception of the pure essence of mind as the light that is the teacher, Buddha Lamp, and praise of him. It is the core of everything, all phenomena and all revelation, where everything is known. This omniscience is personified as the gentle youth, shining in glory. He has no goal to attain and nothing to strive for, so in him nonaction is effortlessly perfected, and without any endeavor he rests in the matrix of pure pleasure.

2 *The Luminous-Mind Modality Is Not Contingent upon a Vow of Moral Conduct*

As the basis of all disciplines, such as moral conduct,
luminous mind provides release in its every mode,
it is buddha's mother and the universal path—
without it buddha could not come into being:
I am the way of supreme liberation.

The pure essence of mind is the foundation of a vast array of behavioral modes, including the disciplines derived from the vow of moral conduct and from the tantric commitments. Insofar as luminous mind is the ground of them all, all of them partake of its liberating function. The pure essence is thus called "the mother of joyful buddha." The all-inclusive path, however, embraces everybody, whether or not they maintain vows of moral conduct. If vows of moral conduct were to lack the modality of release, buddha would not be begotten; but whatever the nature of the conduct, since it is grounded in the pure essence of mind, it possesses the function of release. For this reason, there is no vow of moral conduct in the modality of supreme liberation. It is this freedom that Vajrasattva represents.

The pure essence of mind, as the supreme source, is the origin of all the paths and approaches to buddha and provides simultaneously the modality of release of all those manifold lifestyles. Vajrasattva is the modality of supreme liberation [see *Eternal Victory Banner*, verse 1]. All disciplines and all samaya commitments are assimilated to these aspects of buddha and thus subsumed by Vajrasattva. The process of supreme release, however, is dependent upon no discipline or samaya commitment whatsoever.

3 *The Universal Modality of Liberation Inherent in Luminous Mind Is Inscrutable*

Subtle and elusive, this universal path transcends thinking and
    nonthinking;
without location or reference—indeterminate—it is beyond
    all ideation;
unutterable, it has no color or shape in a sensory field;
intangible and inscrutable, it is inexpressible.

The universal modality of liberation inherent in luminous mind cannot be conceived and transcends thought and thoughtlessness. It has no reference point in any concrete name or form; it cannot be isolated or localized in any way. It is utterly indeterminable and thus cannot be framed as any idea and cannot be expressed verbally. In this way it is subtle and elusive.

4 *The Dangers of the Path of Formal Meditation*
Whoever follows the ancient ascetics' path
becomes sick from attachment to the meditation process;
his teachers' literal instruction construed as a quest,
he chases a stream of concepts, as if pursuing a mirage:
the perfect modality cannot be indicated by words,
and any "true doctrine" is a travesty of Vajrasattva.

Whether Buddhist, Hindu, or Bon, the classical path of meditation is a snare and a delusion when attachment to it becomes obsessive and it becomes an end in itself. The habit of meditation becomes a disease when there is no liberating function in the process. It is a disease when a blissful trance state seemingly separates an arrogant yogin from his mind. But above all it is a disease simply because it is goal-oriented and promises attainment only if the present is prostituted to the future. This state of alienation is caused by mistaking mental constructs for the path, to mistake the shadow of the meaning expressed in words for the thing itself, its heart meaning. The meanings of the words are taken as sacred concepts. The letter of the instruction is taken to heart rather than its spirit. To take the teacher's word literally is, for example, to construe reality as something concrete to be attained by striving in technique and method rather than as a door into the reality of the moment. Words and concepts are a means to their own transcendence in the here and now. Fascination with structure is a deviation; doctrine professed as "true" and "correct" gives Vajrasattva a mask of the ridiculous.

5 *Bewilderment and Ignorance Are the Ground of Enlightenment*
Purity and impurity, as one, indissolubly mixed,
pristine awareness and bewilderment are indivisible;
this is the lamp of unimpeded clarity free of mentation,
and intractable nescience, in itself, is sovereign samadhi.

All the polarities and dichotomies perpetrated by the intellect are resolved in the timeless pristine awareness of luminous mind. What is called "pure" and what is called "impure" are a seamless whole, and what is called "pristine awareness" and what is called "bewilderment" and "ignorance" are precisely the same thing. Both ignorance and pristine awareness reside in luminous mind, and the nature of mind is the nature of all. This unity is the lamp of buddha and the heart of luminous mind, and pristine awareness itself is by definition unimpeded and all penetrating. The state of unmitigated gloom is inherently a state of supreme absorption so that "stupidity" and "languid indifference" are another way of saying "undiscriminating samadhi." [See also *Great Garuda*, verse 19, and *Eternal Victory Banner*, verse 44.]

6 *There Is Nothing to See with the Buddha Eye*

The eye of direct insight seeing directly sees nothing,
and it is called "the buddha eye of omniscience";
know the nature of vastness without center or boundary,
and there lies undiscriminating sovereign sameness.

In the samadhi of pristine awareness there are no points of reference, no image to focus upon, no particularity. The buddha eye of omniscience sees directly into the nature of things, and because that reality has no field of reference, it is said to see nothing or not to see at all. A "soft" expanse without center or circumference is a definition of reality.

7 *Whatever Appears to the Senses Is Pure Enjoyment*

Luminous mind and its habits are one, indissolubly mixed:
all manifest experience, by mind projected,
shines as adornment neither accepted nor rejected—
simply let it be and enjoy it!

In the pure essence of mind, in the natural condition, there is no distinction between mind and its proclivities. So there is no chance to modify or change habits. Whatever appears in the windows of mind—the five sensory windows—is determined by mental habit and constructed by the conditioned mind. But the senses themselves make no distinction between the forms that appear in those windows. They make no judgment of quality or suitability. There is no attribution of good or bad. They do not suppress or reject some forms while letting others in. The indiscriminate senses allow each sensation to arise as aesthetic decoration to be enjoyed in and as itself, regardless of its form. There is absolutely nothing to be done to it. Any intention to change it or modify it precludes the pure enjoyment.

8 No Vice Is Outside the Pale of Luminous Mind

Activity that is anathema or taboo,
the five emotions and the five inexpiable crimes,
deliver sovereign sameness on the path of purity;
nothing is rejected—certainly not sex.

Insofar as proclivities of mind that spontaneously manifest as conventionally repugnant antisocial activity or as passionate emotivity are inseparable from luminous mind, they generate experience not different from any ordinary activity. But since they are accompanied by social disdain, and perhaps personal guilt, they provide a space of alienation in which the sameness of pristine awareness being imperative to sanity is seemingly amplified. In such experience, without seeking to cultivate or abandon it, lies sublime and utter purity, and whoever enters there attains the ultimate sameness of luminous mind. Thus the abodes of desire—in particular the opposite sex—are not to be avoided. This is highlighted in the mahayoga samaya commitments.

Although social taboos vary from society to society, passionate emotivity is universally of five kinds—lustful, angry, jealous, arrogant, and fearful. The five inexpiable crimes are matricide, patricide, arhaticide, creating schism in the community, and maliciously letting the blood of a tathagata, none of which can be absolved, it is said, because the karmic consequences are immediate.

9 The Traditionalist Approaches Are Anathema

The intellect conditioned by traditional form and literal meaning,[15]
the three samadhis[16] **prepared, belief in doctrine and dogma,**
this is all a glitch in the effortless transmission—it is delusion:
abide in the spontaneous pleasure of free-form perfection!

We know history by the forms that tradition passes to us through body language, signs, and symbols, through oral or bardic transmission, and through literature. We also know it by primordial intuition of Samantabhadra and Vajrasattva. When this legacy of tradition is assimilated to the rational mind, tested and proven, when "history" is spun out into a linear, logical pattern through time by intellectual endeavor, the yogin becomes conditioned to the forms and literal meanings of the tradition and loses spontaneity. If the history of philosophy, likewise, discerned in the strata of veils that enshroud momentary pure being, becomes a function of linear logical mind, conditioned by the academic approach, it is delusory. If, meanwhile, he practices the three mahayoga samadhis of "body," "speech," and "mind" with meditative absorption, he cultivates the three modes or dimensions of being (*trikaya*) on a path with a goal in mind. (The three mahayoga samadhis of the here-and-now, the all-illuminating samadhi and the seed syllable samadhi, relate respectively to the three dimensions of essence, nature, and compassion.) Through projection and application of the gendered principles of means and insight, he is lost on a goal-oriented path. Following the established tenets of dogma and doctrine, he may engage in comparative philosophy and even speculative metaphysics; he may even teach it, but he is lost in goal-directed endeavor. This method of traditionalist scholars and conventional intellectuals effectively blankets the momentary effusion of Samantabhadra's spontaneous transmission. Imperative free-form nonaction is lost in the straightjacket of tradition and goal-oriented discipline.

10   Nonaction Is the Natural Condition

The core of sublime self-sprung awareness,
imperturbable, unchanging, unelaborated—
this is the ambrosia of timeless consummation
that vanquishes the pain of any exertion:
every ambition fulfilled, rest in the here and now!

The nature of cognition itself is ultimately fulfilling and forestalls the need to strive for any satisfaction through the strenuous exertion of directed activity. The suffering of failure to obtain what is desired, of obtaining what is undesirable, and of losing what is in hand is all obviated by the elixir of pristine awareness. Since pristine awareness cannot be changed, the here and now is perfect and complete in itself. Even if there is an illusion of evolution, the actuality of the moment is beyond change, so there is no goal to be achieved and nothing to do. The ambrosia of nonduality consummates the activity of every moment: nonaction is the mode in a field of effortless consummation.

Hey, Magnificent Being, listen!
All and everything in experience
has the nature of luminous mind—
it is the all-inclusive seminal nucleus;
incapable of elaboration or concentration,
expansion or contraction,
origination or cessation;
unconfined, it is simply being.
This inconceivable essence,
timelessly present like the sky,
ubiquitous like space,
transcends ideas and speech.[17]

THE ETERNAL VICTORY BANNER:
THE VAST SPACE OF VAJRASATTVA

THE ETERNAL VICTORY BANNER is the source of all transmission and pith instruction. More specifically, it teaches total nonaction, whereby all and everything is already perfect. In this great transmission, Samantabhadra reveals himself to Vajrasattva as his own nature. "I am you," he affirms. "I am luminous mind and luminous mind is the vast space of Vajrasattva."[18]

THE TIMELESS MOMENT OF REALITY

1

The vast space of Vajrasattva,
the all-good expanse of the field of reality,
this is an all-releasing and pure modality,
uncreated, unceasing, and unthinking.

The Sublime Teacher—Samantabhadra
Vajrasattva is the all-pervasive spaciousness of our unchanging being whose exaltation lies in his unalterable self-sprung awareness. His undiscriminating reality is Samantabhadra, the all-good, all-inclusive field of reality, the basic spaciousness that is the dharmadhatu. Everything dissolving into it and emerging from it in unimpeded and relaxed enjoyment, all buddha and sentient beings of the threefold universe (sensual, aesthetic, and formless) are released instantaneously into luminous mind. In this way, nothing substantial in the field of reality is ever created, nothing whatsoever ever comes into existence or ceases to be. Self-sprung awareness lies therein,

unimpeded, in an unrelenting samadhi that has neither beginning nor end, conceiving nothing nor motivating anything at all.

Samantabhadra, who is luminous mind itself, is the perfect teacher of every situation. Disclosing his nature to Vajrasattva, he says, "You are the clear sky of pure awareness, and I, as the teacher, show you my undiscriminating reality. I am luminous mind, and all and everything simultaneously emanates from me and dissolves into me, and in that process lies ineluctable release."[19]

Thus the reality of the teacher, Vajrasattva, is the nature of being.

2

Loving-kindness is already consummate,
so compassion is not pursued;
supremely vast and deep,
no quality exists to acclaim.

The Exaltation of Enlightenment Here and Now
Loving-kindness is the nature of the all-pervasive luminous mind, so it is love itself that has already fulfilled the ultimate goal, which is the ever-immanent reality of Vajrasattva. Compassion is then the nature of reality, as buddha affirms, and it is futile to focus and direct to any being what is already present as his or her nature. It is impossible to cultivate what is naturally already fully potentiated, and so any practice of compassion is redundant. It is counterproductive to allow compassion to become an affective response to extraneous pain, since that would create a dichotomy of inner and outer and an obstacle to spontaneous compassionate flow.

The exaltation of pristine awareness is its immaculate nature, and this can be neither improved nor altered nor conscientiously cultivated nor actualized. Such exaltation is profound because dualistic perception is transcended. In that ulterior nonreferential space where there is no imperfection or blemish, there is no fault to rectify and no flaw to acknowledge, so how can there be any particular quality to extol or any success to celebrate?[20]

Thus Vajrasattva is shown as loving-kindness.

3

Intentions unstirring from their own nature
through nonaction are released and activate release;
unseeking self-sprung awareness,
liberating, reveals the modality of release.

Transmission Ultimately Resolving All Experience

Our identity—our individuality—is the unalterable reality of luminous mind. Not even our intentions and impulses, our aims and objectives, our reactions and responses, can ever escape their natural condition, which is this unalterable reality. By doing nothing at all, through no directed activity, free of endeavor, without striving—which is nonaction—the great perfection is recognized. Pristine awareness, contingent upon neither cause nor condition, liberates itself through its ungrasping natural state and reveals the liberating modality.

To resolve all experience as pure meaning is the purpose of the essential message of the transmission of *The Eternal Victory Banner*: release into the great perfection is inherent in every movement of the mind, whether of buddha or ordinary being, so long as there is no striving to attain it.[21]

Thus the ordinary mind is naturally liberated in the moment. Character and personality are never divorced from luminous mind.

THE TIMELESS MOMENT OF INTRINSIC PRESENCE

4

Vajrasattva is the great elements
intrinsically present in all beings;
even though false notions obsess us,
release is self-sprung—but only in him.

The Consummation of Mahayoga

The totality, Vajrasattva, is universally present as the five "great" elements of earth, water, fire, air, and space, and these elements are fivefold all-creating buddha. All the six kinds of mythic beings—gods, men, titans, hungry ghosts, animals, and hell beings—are composed of these elements. Thus Vajrasattva is a constant, all-embracing presence. We may conceive of the elements in any way—symbolically, personified, materialistically, or functionally—but regardless of any such notions, and despite any conceptualization of Vajrasattva, as fivefold buddha he is the place of ineluctable, spontaneous release.

In mahayoga the five elements are located in the mindstream and visualized as the mandala of fivefold buddha (Vairochana, Akshobhya, Ratnasambhava, Amitabha, and Amoghasiddhi) representing the primordial purity of the five elements. This is a contrived process of goal-oriented meditation. But since the luminous mindstream is the great perfection, it encompasses all such enumerations and all such meditative techniques, and the moment of praxis arises spontaneously as Vajrasattva. Mahayoga provides a door into the great perfection itself when its meditative technique is recognized as embraced by luminous mind.[22]

Thus Vajrasattva is intrinsically, naturally present in the here and now.

THE TIMELESS MOMENT OF NATURAL EXALTATION

5

**Exalted pristine awareness, so elusive,
can be accomplished through means and insight;
although these appear as a supporting extraneous fiction,
real pleasure arises only spontaneously.**

The Consummation of Anuyoga

Pristine awareness is impossible to locate because it has no reference, no address. The difficulty of access may be overcome through recognition of the intrinsic union of reality and pure presence. This would appear to imply a dependence upon an ineffectual nominal duality, but since the exaltation of pristine awareness—immediate pure pleasure—arises only from and in luminous mind, which is quite beyond cause and effect, its nature can only be spontaneity.

In the case of intractable ignorance of the intrinsic perfection of the nature of mind where pristine awareness remains elusive, recourse may be made to the anuyoga construct of means and insight (Tib: *thabs dang shes rab*), which provides a referential address to the pure pleasure of pristine awareness. Skillful means is pure presence (iconographically represented as Samantabhadra, the male principle) and insight is the spaciousness of the field of reality (Samantabhadri, the female principle). Pure pleasure is intrinsic to this timeless primordial union, and spontaneity is its nature. Anuyoga is fulfilled through the great perfection of mind.

All the skillful means of the lower, secondary approaches to mahabodhi arise out of the pure nature of mind, which is perfect and complete in itself and can never be divorced from the pure presence of natural spontaneity. Here Dzogchen is the complete yoga, subsuming all others.

Thus the intrinsical vast presence of luminous mind is shown to encompass the apparent duality of the gendered principles of means and insight.

The Timeless Unsought Moment

6

**The sublime magical illusion is easy to find:
through a subtle understanding of actuality,
of all potential and potency,
it instantly emerges by itself.**

The Consummation of Sattvayoga

Sublime magical illusion, the display of maya, is self-revealing luminous mind. When its nature is understood as uncreated and unstructured, as a totally insubstantial illusion, like a conjuror's trick, it is reflexively attained. Out of the realization of its nature as uncontrived reality, the indestructible potential of pure being and pristine awareness, the vast potential of buddha past, present, and future emerges smoothly without any obstruction as all and everything. The sense of illusion cannot be forced; it is reflexive and innate and cannot be separated from a realization of suchness, the field of reality.

The vision of reality as illusion is a spontaneous revelation that cannot be forced. Nevertheless, this natural process is facilitated in outer yogatantra (*sattvayoga*). The process involves visualization of the qualities of a buddha-deity (*jnana sattva*) and subsequent internalized identification of that as the commitment being (*samaya sattva*). Perception of magical illusion arises spontaneously in that practice. But such meditation is child's play [see also verse 36].

In this verse and the next it is shown that making any effort, any attempt to find the illusive nature of reality, is futile and counterproductive. There is nothing to do!

7

**The invisible nature of reality
fills the mind when searching stops;
stressing about the what and the wherefore
inhibits its spontaneous arising.**

The Fulfillment of Nonmeditation

The delusion of a material environment and the existence of animate beings cannot arise in the perceptual nonduality of luminous mind. This reality is an absence of appearances. Simply by relaxing, unstressed, wanting nothing—which is the supreme meditation of nonmeditation—there it is! The attempt to pin down essentially nonexistent appearances, to insist upon something concrete where nothing substantial exists, to seek any definitive meaning: this is similar to trying to put a solid roof on an imaginary house. Nothing can come of nothing.

Thus searching for something that is already there, and the counter-result of anxious striving, is futile.

The Inexpressible Timeless Moment

8

This hermetically sealed reality[23]
cannot be transmitted to the ear,
and neither has the tongue the power
to express a bit of it.

The Exaltation of Nonenlightenment

The teaching of all-inclusive perfection cannot be expressed by buddha, man, or woman, and so it cannot be transmitted orally. If it cannot be spoken or heard, it does not exist. So what is enlightenment?

Buddha or enlightenment is unattainable, and its reality cannot be taught or expressed. It is beyond mentation, nonreferential, indeterminable, lacks any indication, and is noncomposite. In this sense it does not exist; it is an absence, and in this vast absence lies its exaltation. Nonenlightenment translates as universal enlightenment.

Thus there is no such thing as enlightenment.

The Timeless Moment of Immunity to Karma

9

The suffering of beings is bodhichitta,
and fully awakened, it is song and dance;
unstirring, immovable,
like infinite space, suffering is sameness.

Pith Instruction on Luminous Mind

The pain of each of the six kinds of mythic beings—human beings, gods, titans, hungry ghosts, animals, and devils—is determined by a particular emotional (hormonal) poison, and all of it is the essence of luminous mind. Since it is all-pervading, luminous mind comprehends all pain through the empty dimensions of physical, energetic, and mental emanation, and thereby it is recognized as the wonderful display of pure being and manifold pristine awareness of buddha past, present, and future. The activity of all beings, forever spontaneously arising, the pernicious reactivity of desire, aversion, stupidity, jealousy, pride, and greed, all spontaneously arising forever, all emerges in and is comprehended by the pure essence of mind. It can never become anything but luminous mind. Because luminous mind has the nature of sameness, it suffuses all human suffering and activity equally, just as infinite space permeates all things. [See also verses 15 and 16.]

Human beings can never be irrevocably conditioned by karma—never need be slaves to karma. Luminous mind renders karmic conditioning ineffective and impotent. Karma is denied here as anything but delusory construct of the intellect, karmic product accepted as the illusory basis of the primary Dzogchen method. Experience of the six kinds of mythic beings should be recognized as the primary path. The all-suffusing presence of luminous mind, however, overwhelms karma, rendering it redundant. Karma is, after all, mere imputation.[24]

Thus the wheel of life arises out of luminous mind and always remains luminous mind.

10

We tend to interpret congruous distinctions
as "karmic" relationship;
inasmuch as "karma" holds sway,
self-sprung awareness is lacking.

Perfection Unconditioned by Karma

All pure pleasure of buddha, and the pain and anxiety of ordinary people's passions, are identical as the essence of luminous mind. Yet our equivocal intellect persists in explaining the apparent discrepancy between buddha and sentient beings, and the differences in people's behavior, by reference to the effects of previous actions, and we become enmeshed in a web of mental constructs created by linear, causal thought processes. Thus belief in karma is like an overpowering drug that clouds the mind and inhibits the emergence of pristine awareness. Free of all causes and conditions, pristine awareness arises spontaneously.

Thus it is affirmed that belief in karma is an obstacle to the spontaneous emergence of pristine awareness. The intellect seeks to concretize distinctions and reify illusion by substantiating causal relationship. But thought cannot stir from basic spaciousness.

11

The sole cause, the only condition, is immutable,
and never originating, it can never be destroyed;
in this timeless primordial pure essence of mind,
speculative thought-forms cannot affect basic spaciousness.

Perfection without Recourse

Luminous mind is the universal source, the first cause, the only condition. Like the vajra it is immutable and all victorious. Since it has neither cause nor seed, it is not created; because it has no external condition acting upon it, it is indestructible. This timeless pure essence of mind is immune to mental constructs that seek to condition the mind to causality. Even the most intense speculative thought and potent ideas that seek to structure it, explain it, divulge it, alter it, or pin it down remain mere fluff in the mind, and the field of reality remains unmoving.

Thus it is emphasized that karma is a concept imposed upon immaculate uncaused reality and, like any thought-form, is ineffectual in altering the natural perfection of the luminous-mind reality in any way. Karmic patterning, as mental construct, is ineffective.

THE TIMELESS MOMENT OF MENTAL EFFORT

12

Concentration in its finest form
is nonreflective in its very nature;
as unreflected, unaltered experience,
pristine awareness arises in thought itself.

The Glitch of Concentrated Absorption

Nonmeditation includes and transcends all positive and negative veils, even the obscuring trance qualities that arise in meditative absorption. These trance qualities, including imperturbability, clarity, bliss, serenity, resplendence, pristine awareness–suffused mind, and extrasensory perception, become glitches and veils only when they are objectified. But the natural concentration inherent in meditative absorption is free of perceptual dualism and automatically subsumes these trance qualities. This finest, natural concentration is nonreflective and incapable of ideation. So why strive to attain thoughtlessness? In the nonmeditation of natural concentration, discursive thought itself, left alone, unaltered, effloresces as pristine awareness. In the simple natural state of concentration that is unthought and thoughtless, the nature of emergent thought is pristine awareness itself. Naturally perfect meditation—nonmeditation—is free of all motivation and mental striving. Pristine awareness arises in thought itself, thus meditative absorption is redundant.

Glitches in the Dzogchen modality are a function of a delusive dualism that produces mental effort. While the slightest endeavor in the face of a complete absence of motivation and striving in luminous mind is folly, nevertheless that folly is naturally pure and perfect in itself and arises in a timeless moment of mental exertion.[25]

Thus thought and mental constructs themselves are pristine awareness.

13

Some identify luminous mind as a subtle door:
seeking a way to isolate it,
they fixate on the voidness of the mindstream—
if it is contrived it is conceptual meditation.

The Glitch of Subtle Method

There is no perceptual dualism in nonmeditation, but within the consciousness that constructs subjective and objective elements in sensory perception, luminous mind can be conceived as the door of liberation—something infinitely subtle but still concrete. In a dualistic frame, luminous mind is thus regarded as an entrance into a higher state and not the starting point: the path and the goal rolled into one. Based on such an idea, in physical isolation, free of intrusive energy forms, meditation becomes a method of putting the sensory fields and mental activity into abeyance through a very fine samadhi of voidness. When the chakras of "body," "speech," and "mind" are visualized in such meditation techniques, they also are subtly concretized. Such technique is always contrived and goal-oriented in nature. Any meditation that involves intellectual activity, such as focusing on a particular aspect of mind or visualization, however subtle, and any meditation that can be deconstructed, is conceptual in nature.[26]

Thus luminous mind, which lacks any impulse to seek itself, inveigles itself into subtle meditative endeavor.

14

Some believe that by designating cause and effect,
both virtue and vice are clearly defined
and the mundane world is transcended;
moral discrimination is supreme presumption!

The Glitch of Moral Discrimination

To designate moral cause and effect is to create a self-contained and self-fulfilling system of behavior and reward. What is defined as virtue invariably produces a positive result and what is defined as vice a negative result. In this life the happiness of heaven and the upper realms is the effect of virtuous behavior, and the misery of hell and the lower realms is the result of negative activity. Through the moral discipline of cultivating virtuous activity and forsaking vice the suffering of the world is transcended.

When one is familiar with the moral-causal process and skilled in the discipline of moral discrimination, the result of any action can be predicted; but this facility may produce enormous complacence and arrogance that can result in exclusivity and intolerance. As a solution to the problem of existence, furthermore, this analysis is incompatible with the pure-luminous-mind modality, wherein the conception and the consonant action are simultaneous: the conception consisting of luminous-mind reality and the action as nonaction. There is no duality of cause and effect in luminous mind.

The path of moral conduct as a method of liberation is contrary to the luminous-mind principle of nonaction and absence of endeavor. Goal-oriented purveyors of karmic cause and effect entrap themselves in exclusive complacency. Yet thought itself is pristine awareness.

Thus this verse shows that even moralists are encompassed by the great perfection.

THE TIMELESS MOMENT OF SEAMLESS NONDUALITY

15

The words "attachment" and "detachment,"
as in the middle way, are but echo,
and pleasure and pain are basically the same.
The lord of beings, Vajrasattva, said that.

Unequivocal Congruence of Pleasure and Pain
Desire focuses upon an imaged object in the sensory fields, where attachment arises. But since the sensory fields have no substance and can be said to have no existence, desire and attachment have no real objective. In this sense neither attachment nor detachment are real; they appear only as indices in mere wordplay. In the middle way all sound is but echo; investigating "attachment" and "detachment" as mere sound, both are similar music to the ear.

Furthermore, the realities of pleasure and pain, happiness and suffering, and the five passions are identical in the pure essence of mind. Here "identity" means causal identity, which in the Dzogchen context means their real identity in and as luminous mind; the labels "pleasure" and "pain" refer to their nominal distinction in dualistic perception. Vajrasattva is sovereign lord of the six kinds of mythic beings of the six realms insofar as he is the nature of the elements that compose them.[27] [See verses 4 and 46.]

Thus the great perfection is seamless and flawless in nondual vision.

THE TIMELESS MOMENT OF SELF-SPRUNG AWARENESS

16

Vajrasattva says:
Desire, anger, and bewilderment
also occur in the sublime luminous-mind modality;
and the five sensual pleasures
ornament the spaciousness that is the field of reality.

Exaltation of the Enlightened Field of Reality

The reality of luminous mind is the field of reality of Samantabhadra, the basic spaciousness that is the dharmadhatu. The potential pollutants on the luminous-mind path are desire, hatred, and bewilderment; these three tendencies—positive, negative, and neutral—are immediately integrated into enlightened existential reality through the buddha modes of "body," "speech," and "mind" respectively. The five sensual pleasures of our usual behavior—sight, sound, smell, taste, and tactile sensation—which are most potent in sensual-sexual situations, are then adornments of that field of reality, like small baskets of flowers tossed onto the surface of a stream. They are instantaneously integrated as pure being and pristine awareness. In this way indulgence in sensual pleasure is the luminous-mind modality itself, and enjoyment is its mode.

Pristine awareness arises spontaneously in desire, aversion, and bewilderment, which are objects of the internal senses, and also in the five sensual pleasures, which are the objects of the five external senses. Thus basic spaciousness is always enlightened [see also verse 44]. The exaltation of the field of reality as already enlightened is elaborated in terms of Vajrasattva as the five great elements [see verses 4 and 47].

Thus passion and sensual pleasure are the path.

17

Space and the concept of space are both unoriginated,
so the concept itself is just like space;
in the detachment of dedicated space,
ultimate self-validating space emerges.

The Reality of Dzogchen Anuyoga

The reality of anuyoga is the vajra sensory fields. The thought of space, like space itself, has no substance or origin and is therefore said to be unoriginated and unstructured, which is the nature of the field of reality. Constructs and concepts—all thought forms—arise in the mind-sky like clouds or miasma. Their particularity never comes into existence. They remain utterly without structure, as is the nature of the field of reality. Concepts are therefore like space. Like concepts, the five sensual pleasures—form, sound, smell, taste, and touch—are seen as neutral, desire-free space; through the idea that everything is space emerges all-inclusive spaciousness, which is thick with its own heart meaning.

There can be no attachment to conceptualized pure being (dharmakaya) due to its illusory spacious nature. All concepts are dedicated as space, but conceptual pure being in particular—the pure being of "body," "speech," and "mind," and of "past," "present," and "future"—is seen as space; the reality of pure being is realized as self-validating space, which is the ultimate purpose. This is an analysis of a spontaneous, instantaneous process.

Here is described the modality wherein the six sensory fields are recognized as the reality of luminous mind—the vajra sensory field. This recognition is accomplished by their "dedication" as space. Here *dedication* means "the projection of the idea of space upon constructs arising in the sensory fields and thereby actualizing their inherent spacious reality." It describes thought forms and sensual pleasure arising spontaneously as pristine awareness. There is no gap between the intention and the action. The process occurs within the spontaneity of self-sprung awareness. The notion of "dedication" assigns this momentary reality to anuyoga.[28]

Thus recognition of the spaciousness of concepts actuates the great perfection.

THE TIMELESS MOMENT OF UNION WITH THE CONSORT

18

Unthought sameness, pure being,
like the moon's reflection in water, cannot be grasped;
in the all-good display of Samantabhadra,
it is revealed as the ulterior vowels and consonants.

The Perfection of Samantabhadra's Display

The reality of luminous mind is like space; mind, unthinking and without constructs, is the sameness of pure being (dharmakaya). Within pure being, actuality lacks any concrete name or form whatsoever—it is utterly insubstantial—so there is nothing to grasp and hold on to. Within the unoriginated pure being of Samantabhadra, the magical illusion of creation is apparent and all of creation is Samantabhadra's display. Inasmuch as this display of reality is like the reflection of the moon in water, it cannot be grasped. That is the reality of immediate phenomenal manifestation.

The phantasmagoria of Samantabhadra's display is a revelation of an interior language. The vowels of this language represent its unborn, unstructured nature; the consonants, the pure presence that can never be crystalized. The intermingling of vowels and consonants in a moment of nondual experience of the totality is called "union with the mudra, or consort." The union of the reality of luminous mind (the vowels) and presence (the consonants) is primordial and timeless—there is no method or technique to facilitate it. In the anuyoga of the previous verse, this union is to be recognized in the spaciousness of concepts as well as in sensual pleasure.

Thus the unity of language and the form of the magical display is revealed.[29]

19

As the *a* and the adorning *ta*,
as the *pa* and its complex elaborations,
as the field of experience of the finite world,
ulterior buddha speech emerges.

Direct Transmission—Emanation in the Nature of Mind
Samantabhadra's pure being (dharmakaya) in luminous-mind reality (dharmadhatu) is defined by the glyph *a*, which is pure potential, and the glyph *ta*, which is the potentiation. The glyph *pa* describes the entire elaborate miraculous emanation within pure being. The aggregates of this magical display are the subjective functions of mind (name and form, feeling, perception, volition, and consciousness). The eight forms of consciousness (five sensory and three mental) are secondary emanations that embrace the entire field of multifarious experience of the finite world. Within that field, the five sensual pleasures of the five emotions are the energy patterns of buddha past, present, and future, and they are known as buddha speech. Thus the uncreated luminous mind reality of form, sound, smell, and so on is ulterior buddha speech, just because it is uncreated.

Buddha speech may be interpreted as vibration or as energy patterns, but in this description of the process of emanation within pure being, such energy constellations are formalized as alphabetic glyphs. The glyph *pa* is the first letter of the word *padma*, the embryonic sound, the generative organ. Out of *pa* arise the vowels and consonants each corresponding to an aspect of emanation—the five aggregates, the eight types of consciousness, the five emotions, the five sensual pleasures, and so on—and in the complexity of sensual, aesthetic, and formless experience in the field of reality, they spell the whole gamut of possible activity. Since the reality of sensual pleasure is uncreated, it is the ulterior voice of buddha. Since reality is unborn the content of the moment is buddha teaching.

Aspects of emanation consist of the five aggregates, the eight types of consciousness (consciousness of the five external and three internal senses), the five emotions (desire, anger, pride, jealousy, and fear), the five sensual pleasures (sight, sound, taste, touch, and sensation), the five sense fields, and so on.

Thus union with the consort is described.

20

No! the field of buddha experience
cannot be found by seeking and striving;
as sixfold sensory experience provides no object,
to seek it is like a blind man reaching for the sky.

The Glitch of Striving

A serious deviation from Dzogchen praxis is to search for what is spontaneously and ineluctably present. Pure being and pristine awareness, which comprise the marvelous field of buddha experience, are contingent upon nothing. The field itself is instantaneously self-sprung. Any attempt to grasp the desirable and fascinating objects of the senses is bound to be frustrated because nothing substantial is there. The impulse to reach out to grasp the six objects of consciousness (which comprise "sixfold experience") derives from a delusive perceptual dualism. It is as futile and foolish as a blind man stretching up his arms in order to grasp the sky.

Thus there is danger in striving for a product. To do so is an error in behavior. The union with the consort (the field of buddha experience) is naturally perfected in the here and now, and no technique or effort can facilitate it.

21

The path of purity reaching from height to height
is at odds with the free-form modality;
journeying on the pathless path,
as in boundless space, there is no destination.

The Glitch of Belief in Progress on a Path

The yogin who believes that the path of buddha, the luminous-mind process, is a graduated path is sidetracked onto a structured path of levels and stages. There are no stages in the Dzogchen modality; there are no degrees of attainment. A graduated path of purification is incompatible with effortless spontaneity in which there is no endeavor; this is the path of imperative nonaction. Utter relaxation on an unstructured path does not allow for striving toward a structured goal. If there were progress on the Dzogchen path it would be an endless process, and if there were any destination it would be the ever-receding horizon. On a graduated path, to the contrary, each moment is the destination, and there is no other goal.

Thus to deviate from the luminous-mind modality to a graduated path is a potential error.

THE TIMELESS MOMENT OF COMPLETE PERFECTION

22

Because things are perfect just as they are,
in the moment of revelation lies the attainment;
the essence of luminous mind is the universal source,
and the entire reality is pure and simple. Yes!

The Aural Transmission

Things are pure and simple just as they are because in the all-good, immutable reality of Samantabhadra there is no such thing as evolution, development, or progress. Only the one reality is continuously present. Whatever appears momentarily in the mind-sky is the complete goal, the ultimate totality.

In the modality of oral transmission whatever is taught and revealed in the moment is ineluctably realized in the moment by whoever is capable. The attainment is intrinsic to the momentary efflorescence, and the revelation and attainment are simultaneous in the same way that the pure essence of mind is at once indeterminate reality itself and the source of reality.

Thus the moment is totally perfect and complete, and source and reality have a suprarational identity. This and the following two verses treat complete perfection, the all-inclusive intrinsic perfection of the here and now.

23

What was before and what is now
as suchness is the same intrinsic vastness;
such is the buddha modality
for suchness is its nature.

The Perfection of the Path

The past is known only through the thought constructs of memory, which in reality are luminous mind. The present is the basic spaciousness of the field of reality known as pristine awareness. The future, like the past, is known only as mental constructs or projections, which, again, are in reality luminous mind. The actuality, the thing-in-itself, the suchness of past, present, and future, is an identical vast and spacious presence. The buddha modality through which the past is known does not differ from the modality by which the future is known, and neither differ from the present modality, which is unstructured reality itself. Past, present, and future are all known in the here and now, and this buddha modality through which they are understood is a singularity.

24

So the here and now is the whole process,
like the moon and its reflection at one;
yet being entirely the same,
it cannot be seen by a selective focus.

An Image of the Process

The universal process, all-inclusive, is buddha reality. It embraces everyone, knowing and unknowing, and all experience, because the process itself is reality. Reality is like the moon in the sky and its reflection in water made one; like the identity of the moon and the finger pointing at the moon; like the identity of the moon and its verbal indicator. The ultimate sameness of buddha and sentient beings is the pure-pleasure reality that is invisible insofar as it is unobjectified. If we focus upon a single object of the senses as if it were a concrete entity, in a fixed, directed gaze that is partial in that it is selective, this ultimate sameness remains elusive.

Thus the nature of the reality process is shown. The previous verse first does so from the point of view of buddha past, present, and future, where experience of it is identical, while this verse describes its nature as all-inclusive, embracing both buddha and all living creatures.

THE TIMELESS MOMENT OF DESIRELESSNESS

25

**Present pleasure and future pleasure
are direct perception and its shadow:
such conceptual calculation is a mistake—
do not trust in it.**

Unpredictable Pristine Awareness

To believe that a moment of transcendent happiness will automatically lead to another because the present moment of direct perception is the "front side" of pristine awareness whereas the next moment is its "backside" is an error. To attribute "front" and "back" or any relational attribution to pristine awareness is a glitch in the process. To calculate any aspect of luminous mind's pristine awareness is to invite disaster, as calculation implies dependence upon fictional constructs such as past and future.

The notion of a "shadow" of direct perception is derived from attachment to its pure pleasure and hope for repeated pleasure. Attachment to the memory of bliss can generate delusive supportive constructs, like "past" and "future," which undermine the awareness in which bliss is naturally inherent. Pristine awareness transcends all such attachment and is equivocal therefore in that it defies prediction.

Thus the detachment, or desirelessness, in pristine awareness is demonstrated.

THE TIMELESS MOMENT OF PRIMORDIAL VASTNESS

26

**Past, present, and future are one, without distinction,
the past never arisen, the future never arising;
embraced by pure being, all is one,
immanent, an exalted vastness.**

The Unequivocal Unity of Time

In buddha mind, only the here and now pertains. In pristine awareness there has never been any past and there never will be any future. The unity of here and now precludes the possibility of time. It is only the mental habits of human beings that create discrete past, present, and future. Within pure being's unity of time, in the pristine awareness of exalted reality, is spontaneous pure pleasure. Without unity of time, the pure pleasure of immanent reality is not present.

Thus the primordial timelessness of the exalted essence of luminous mind is disclosed. [See verse 24.]

THE TIMELESS MOMENT OF FREEDOM FROM ASPIRATION AND AMBITION

27

With full involvement in the threefold universe,
ideas appear as delusory enchantment;
even the seat of the universal emperor
is a place conditioned by illusion.

The Utter Perfection of the Mundane World

Fully engaged in the world, we are motivated by happiness and profit, fame and reputation, and committed to the pleasures of the senses, aesthetic appreciation, and perhaps to high ideals. Here, phenomena are ultimately uncreated and uncaused, but they appear in a relative universe where ideas determine their illusory form and experience is known through verbal constructs. The whole is a web of delusory enchantment (*maya*). Insofar as that engagement is a purifying process, the merit accumulated in the relative world may lead to a seat of power, or even to the throne of the universal emperor. But that, also, is illusion.

The natural perfection of the threefold universe—the sky, the earth, and the underworld—is a given, even when there is active and committed engagement therein and regardless of the eminence and power status achieved by accumulation of merit. Luminous mind is inescapable. Further, all mundane aspirations and desires, regardless of their fulfillment, are subsumed by luminous mind, and nothing can escape it. But the illusions of power—physical, economic, military, political, spiritual—have no credibility, and maya, illusion, is the one cause for humor.

Thus complete perfection regardless of action or intent is asserted.

28

Those whose lives are slaves of time
never see an immediate outcome;
if activity is fraught with hope,
it can only be "empty" action.[30]

The Utter Perfection of Mundane Motivation

If we conduct our lives on a strict schedule, believing in the future, setting goals now for later attainment, no goal can arise in the present. Insofar as the present is continuously prostituted to the future, no goal can ever be achieved in the present. Serving time means never seeing a goal achieved in the moment. Yet our daily round, our schedule of events, is dependent upon a fictional construct of the future, which in nature is an absence, and thus the here and now is always with us. Even though our daily agendas are fraught with desire and motivated by ambition, even though our goals are located in a nonexistent future unattainable, even as we try to reify emptiness as a concrete achievement, our activity remains forever emptiness. In exertion motivated by desire, emptiness lies in the absence of a result or a product. Knowing emptiness as an absence, rather than as an inherent quality, an intrinsic nature, actuates the perfection of the moment—appearances and existence are empty of everything else, not empty in themselves.

This verse shows that the inherent perfection of the moment can be actuated even when the discursive planning mind is forever running into a nonexistent future. It indicates that past, present, and future—particularly mental constructs relating to the future—are inescapably embraced by luminous mind.

Thus, even though our desires create a counterproductive dependence on time and we hold concrete notions of past and future, there is, nevertheless, automatic access to luminous mind.

THE TIMELESS MOMENT OF TRANSMISSION REVEALED

29

Utterly free of image, as one,
the yogin is like the imprint of a bird in the sky;

in the unstructured, unborn essence,
where is any vaunted sign of his passage?

The Revelation of All Things As One—The Root of All Experience
The nature of mind and luminous mind is one, completely free of any form
and, in particular, free of any temporal attribute—an incalculable singularity. The yogin knows the nature of mind quite beyond its fabrications and
fictions; his pure presence is like an imprint of a bird in the sky and his mastery of the flow is like the flight path of a bird; his reality is like unthinking
space. The pure essence of mind is as empty and unstructured as the imprint
of a bird in the sky since it has no cause and is free of all conditions. Everything whatsoever occurs in pure essence of mind. Yet nothing whatsoever
is substantial there, and nor is there any evidence of something or nothing.
Nothing arises from any cause, nothing is created by any condition, so from
the beginning luminous mind is free of all biased judgment imputing reality here and delusion there, truth here and a lie there, significance here and
futility there, inflating this meaning and deflating that. The yogin leaves no
trace of his achievement or the manner by which it was accomplished, no
doctrine or dogma, no signs or indications. Here, the transmission is the
one nature of mind—all buddha teaching is the one nature of mind.

Every moment and every experience is the inspired revelation of
Samantabhadra. No revelation has any greater significance than any other.
Everything is transmission and there is no specific "Dharma path," just the
all-inclusive modality. The image of the yogin as the flight path of a bird
may be considered a koan, the inconceivable construct that silences the
mind and identifies it with infinite space, and this may constitute a transmission of the singularity of luminous mind.

Thus there is transmission of nonspecific unity.

30

Inner and outer are one, the inner the outer itself,
so there are no hidden depths to discover;
under the power of the fictive world,
samadhi lacks ultimate sameness.

Nondifferentiation of Inner and Outer
The chalice and the elixir, the vessel and the content, body and mind, and
so on are inseparable, the one a mere proposition of the other. Therefore no

hidden—or "inner"—dimension exists to be known. Exoteric and esoteric are indivisible. Everything is up front and in our faces. If we are bewitched by the verbal designations of mental fabrication and we labor under the delusion that there is an esoteric "inner" reality to discover, then the essential quality of sameness will remain elusive. Belief in the dichotomy of inner and outer locks the yogin in a conceptual trap. Conversely, the samadhi that realizes the identity of inner and outer, because neither inner nor outer actually exist, recognizes universal sameness in luminous mind.

In luminous mind our inner and outer lives are one, because the outer itself is the inner and the inner the nature of the outer, and there nothing is hidden or covert. What has significance is the here and now—which is totally complete in itself. This identification of outer and inner applies also to public and private lives. Complete transparency and invisibility are par for the course.

Thus transmission has no dimension, and what you see is what you get.

31

And again about "outer" and "inner,"
the body-mind is undifferentiated space;
past, present, and future inseparable within it,
all such designations are redundant.

Spatial and Temporal Unity
In the samadhi that is utterly free of mental constructs, "outer" and "inner" cannot be computed. They cannot be identified and no distinction can be made between them. They cannot be differentiated. Thus if the psycho-organism, the body-mind, composed of the five aggregates (name and form, feeling, perception, volition, and consciousness) is what is referred to by "outer," as an indeterminable and incalculable reality, it is only present as the "inner" indeterminable element of space. If "inner" refers to the sense fields (the sense organs and their objects and the consciousness of each), again, outer and inner are inseparable, as nothing is there but undifferentiated space. Further, through time, indefinable reality cannot be separated from its spaciousness. So it is specious to say "This is the inner" and "That is the outer." No such designation can be made.

In the Vajrayana, the samayas and commitments are divided into inner and outer sections. We pledge to sustain awareness of the aggregates of the psycho-organism as buddha and the components of the sense fields as bodhisattvas. Since no distinction can be made between the outer aggregates and inner space, or the outer senses and inner space, and since there is no distinction between past, present, and future, spatial and temporal unity obtains, and even the word "commitment" is redundant.[31]

Thus the transmission has spatial and temporal unity.

THE TIMELESS MOMENT OF SAMENESS

32

The immovable is the seal of pure being,
the imperturbable is pristine awareness;
appropriating nothing, there is no self,
rejecting nothing, unutterable sameness.

Complete Perfection of Being and Awareness

Luminous mind never becomes any thing, never becomes any shape, size, or color. Therefore insofar as it never moves out of its own nature, it is immovable and unchangeable, and as such it is called the seal of pure being, which is free of perceptual duality. The self-sprung awareness of pure being remains constant in an imperturbable samadhi. In nondual perception nothing is appropriated from reality, because there is no thing to take and no self to do the grasping and capturing. Refusing nothing, rejecting nothing, everything that arises in the mind fully accepted without discrimination, there is no repression. Through immovability, imperturbability, and nondiscrimination, we can say, "Unutterable, nonverbal, sameness!"

The *immovable* is ultimate, immutable sameness of all experience in terms of pure being or the inherent absence of structure to reality, and the *imperturbable* is the pristine awareness of pure being. The former is the mudra or consort of the latter in a primordial and timeless union. In another context, immovable luminous mind is represented as Achala (or, in Tibetan, Miyowa) and imperturbable samadhi is Akshobhya (or Mikyopa). [This union of pure being and pristine awareness is also treated in verses 6 and 20.]

33

The what, who, and where—
our psychic modes and behavior—occur in luminous mind;
but of any distinction between male and female,
the Lord of Sameness has nothing to say.

Exaltation of Enlightened Identity

The seeming specifics of our lives, who and what we are, our mental environments and psychological states, our dominant passions, the karmic drives that determine our behavior, the various forms of acting out as gods, titans, hungry ghosts, animals, hell-beings, and humans—all this is luminous mind itself and pure essence of mind. Samantabhadra, the personification of the pure essence of mind, makes no mention in the Dzogchen tantras of any distinction between man and woman in his all-inclusive space of sameness and implies, therefore, no gender distinction in the luminous-mind modality.

Thus the sameness of character, that of personality and that of gender, is the ultimate sameness of luminous mind.

THE TIMELESS MOMENT OF DETACHMENT FROM BLISS

34

Renunciation and fierce asceticism
provide no definitive answer;
but endowed with the *a* and the *pa*,[32]
the pleasure of delusory enchantment is assured.

The Immanent Perfection of Renunciation

In the reality where there is nothing to find, if we seek to discipline the six senses through monastic privation or self-mutilating asceticism, no certain result can be achieved and no place to settle can be found. In this state of indeterminacy, however, the disciples (*shravakas*), who elude suffering through renunciation, may experience the fleeting pleasure of delusory enchantment. In the terms of atiyoga (which are not accepted by the disciples), when endowed with the glyph *a*, which represents the conduit of the transmission and provides access to the level of the teacher, also present is the glyph *pa*, which represents the illusory emanation that provides the pleasure.

This ambiguous verse thus serves to demonstrate the perfection immanent in the disciples' renunciant method whereby the glyphs *a* and *pa* may be the occasion for pure pleasure while receiving instruction. On the surface, however, it appears to treat tantrayoga. Practice of relentless asceticism, providing an equivocal, indeterminate space, allows the bliss of the great siddhi to arise in the yoga of union. Attachment to this bliss is pre-empted, however, by the intrinsic union of the glyphs *a* and *pa*, representing luminous mind as coincident source and manifestation [see verse 19].

Thus attachment to the bliss is avoided.

35

Due to the indeterminacy of oneness,
however it is perceived so it appears:
the pleasure coveted in appearances,[33]
this is a heavy obscuring veil.

The Equivocal Nature of Experience

In the Mahayana sutras, it is said that phenomenal appearances are like the reflection of the moon in water. They are like optical illusions, mirages, dreams, echos, fairy castles in the sky, hallucinations, rainbows, lightning, water bubbles, and reflections in a mirror. Through appropriate contemplation, phenomena indeed appear like that. Thus the perceiver's gaze, conditioned by karmic proclivities, determines the form of experience. In this way indeterminate luminous mind appears as it is perceived or in whatever way it is conditioned.

Striving to positively determine the nature of appearances that are infinitely variable prevents the pleasure in the nature of mind. When pleasure is the quality that is sought after in indeterminate experience—which is usually the case—the pleasure that is a projection imposed by mental habit, the striving for it obscures the pleasure innate in all appearances. To covet and hanker after pleasure is self-defeating. In nondual perception there is no object to focus upon, but when mental habit defines a part of that totality as a potential source of pleasure, it is objectified, and the pleasure in the great siddhi of nondual realization vanishes. Obsession with an externalized mental projection is an egregious glitch in the Dzogchen modality.

Attachment to a seemingly existent quality "out there" is implicit in desire for a sexual object. Accepting the nonexistent nature of all phenomena and experience, and understanding them to be the insubstantial though seemingly concrete projections of our mental habits, that attachment is broken.

Thus we are warned against projecting appearances that merely serve to satisfy desire.

36

The method of tantric luminous-mind practice
requires visualization of divine attire
as the moon's reflection in water;
nakedness and detachment emerge—
but this meditation is like building sandcastles.

The Reality of Tantrayoga

The technique employed in the innumerable methods of outer yogatantra
(tantrayoga) is visualization of symbolic forms. In this practice, with the
intellect, a buddha-deity is visualized along with his color, symbolic tokens,
and mudras, and in a mental trance the pellucid though illusory vision
appears. Then the buddha-deity as a being of pristine awareness (*jnana-
sattva*), stripped of all dualistic marks and signs and detached from any sense
of self, unites with the desireless yogi. But this outer yogatantra meditation
is like building sandcastles: a childish, futile pursuit. Pristine awareness is
realized with desirelessness, but it is dependent upon an intellectual exercise
that must be repeated again and again as the vision repeatedly collapses.

Thus it is evident that the practice of yogatantra may induce the bliss of
mahasiddhi, but the bliss is a function of technique and therefore fleeting.

37

Identifying with the body of Mahakrodha
in his mandala of wrathful attributes,
even if the seed syllable is actualized,
nirvana itself cannot be seen directly.

The Reality of Creative Mahayoga

In mahayoga meditation, the mandala of consciousness is visualized with
the visionary attributes of divine wrath with the wrathful deity Mahakrodha at the center. After repeated practice, identifying with the visualized
body of Mahakrodha, the deity actually manifests. Then the seed syllable
hung, matured by habit, may emerge, and thereby the wide-open, uncontrived nature, which is ultimate peace and serenity, is discovered. This is
not the same thing, however, as perceiving nirvana through direct sensory
perception. Mahayoga brings the yogin to the point of nirvana only within
his formal samadhi.

In this verse the bliss of the great siddhi is realized through mahayoga mandala visualization and the actualization of the syllable *hung*. In the great perfection, attachment is preempted by understanding of the limited nature of this mahayoga siddhi.

Thus mahayoga is a contrived meditation technique that leads the way to Dzogchen Ati.

38

Under the sway of emotion,
by lopping the top off the tree,
or incinerating the seed,
its tyranny may be avoided:
so it is taught.

Undiminishing, Inviolable Perfection

The discipline and vows of hermits, disciples, and sutra bodhisattvas deteriorate under the influence of emotion. Their way of dealing with passion—suppression and sublimation ("cutting the top off the palm tree"), or applying an appropriate antidote—is thus thwarted and there is no advantage. In the Vajrayana, the homeopathic method of eradicating the root cause of passion ("incinerating the seed") is futile if the samaya commitments are not maintained. On the other hand, because the Dzogchen samaya commitment is unformed and therefore unbreakable, it provides immunity to all external and internal conditions.

It is folly to attempt to destroy attachment and the foundation of emotion when under the sway of passion. In the graduated process of eradicating emotion, passion is still present to undermine the commitments that are the sole protection against backsliding. The Dzogchen samaya commitment that is no samaya, the spontaneous perfection of the moment, guarantees that it can never deteriorate or degenerate.

Thus attachment to the bliss of the mahasiddhi arising within the practice of the yoga of union on the tantric path is shown to be avoided through the Dzogchen samayas.

39

Each of the hundred thousand techniques
bears an appropriate flower,
but unmarked, signless, perfection
has no particular abode.

The Perfecting Nature of Mind—The Perfection of All Paths

Where there is a technique, a causal process, and a practice, there is a goal, a product, and an effect. Although the goal be even so subtle a state of mind as bliss, if it can be found it can also be lost. But since all methods and all goals arise within the luminous mind that is complete perfection, they cannot but partake of the nature of purity. Dzogchen, however, is an unmarked path, and there is no sign of attainment—not even a small flower. Conversely, due to the signlessness of Dzogchen reality, which is emptiness, the abodes of the pleasure-seeking world cannot emerge under its power, and the heavenly abodes, or trance states, created by meditation techniques cannot appear. Still, the myriad techniques of tantra and the lower approaches continue to be embraced by the pure and perfect nature of mind.

Thus the signlessness of the Dzogchen modality precludes the emergence of attachment to the pleasure of union and desire for mundane happiness.

THE TIMELESS MOMENT OF EFFORTLESSNESS

40

**Present here with a silent mind,
the yogin is fortunate indeed;
self and other indistinguishable,
he revels in the arena of enchanted spontaneity.**

Evidence of Enlightenment

The yogin's mind is silent insofar as all the evaluative and judgmental discussion within himself is transcended in the luminous-mind reality. He knows the unstructured, unfabricated nature of it, and his activity and his compassionate mind come together. In this lies his great fortune; the pleasure that arises without a cause is totally adventitious. With a silent mind, in the pure potential of space, he has nothing to do for himself, and with nothing to urge him to act, he has nothing to do for others. His reality is an enchanted illusion, spontaneously, effortlessly occurring, and there he plays in a natural field of reality. In a state of blissful enchantment, the yogin embodies the exaltation of buddha here and now.

Thus an image of effortless, undirected action is presented affirming the natural authenticity of buddha.

The Timeless Moment of Unchanging Reality

41

**Totally complete, all-inclusive,
unchanging, it is simply being;
and like unbounded space,
reality is contingent upon nothing.**

The Sublime Teaching—The Great Perfection

Samantabhadra is the constant and universal teacher and luminous mind is the timeless teaching. Everything that is revealed is disclosed by Samantabhadra; what is disclosed is always luminous mind. Luminous mind is the great perfection, the essence of all experience, and everything is always all-inclusive, nothing wanting, complete and perfect in itself. Nothing need ever be done—indeed nothing can be done—to improve or alter experience. It is self-sufficient, so it can never be dependent upon anything or anyone else. It is immutable and unchangeable, so no progress is possible. It is always up front and in our faces, so there is nothing hidden that is to be disclosed. Complete and perfect, it is without cause or effect, so nothing is dependent upon anything else.

Thus we are provided a celebration of the great perfection.

42

**Pure pleasure arises spontaneously
and solely and exclusively as pristine awareness
in the potency of pure presence;
reality cannot be anywhere else.**[34]

The Reality of Dzogchen Atiyoga

Pure presence is self-cognition, the yoga of Dzogchen Ati. Freedom from causality and conditioning is the environment in which spontaneity occurs: naturally potent, self-sprung awareness. The nature of pristine awareness is incommensurate with any seemingly concrete name and form, inimical to it. Thus experience, which is pure pleasure, occurs only in spontaneous pure presence.

Pure pleasure is the magical radiance in pure presence of luminous mind's pristine awareness. Its spontaneity indicates an absence of all causal and conditional factors. Luminous mind is all-inclusive and utterly autonomous, and its pristine awareness, naturally self-sprung, transcends every causal process and immediately dissolves any delusory name and form. Timeless spontaneity is the seal of Dzogchen Ati.

Thus the timeless blissful spontaneity of the primal awareness of pure presence is the reality of Dzogchen Ati and is intrinsic to all experience, which can be nothing other than pure pleasure.

43

Easy and difficult, difficult because so easy,[35]
luminous mind, invisible, is all-pervasive;
it cannot be pointed out by name—
even Vajrasattva cannot show it.

Unequivocal Absence of Any Indication of Attainment

In the sense that luminous mind has no cause or condition and is time-lessly, spontaneously present, it is unavoidable and inevitable and therefore easy of access. But since there is no trace of its presence, never an object of focus, never a finite quality, it is impossible to conceptualize and therefore impossible to access. There is no word or definition big enough to identify it because it embraces the entire phenomenal world. Even Vajrasattva himself cannot particularize it or pin it down. For this reason, facility in it cannot be evaluated.

Thus since luminous mind is inseparable from direct perception, it cannot be accessed and yet neither can it be eluded.

THE TIMELESS MOMENT UNCAUSED AND UNCONDITIONED

44

This marvelous, miraculous display,
undirected, free-form, like space,
arises momentarily, spontaneously,
even out of amorphous bewilderment.

The Perfection of Self-Sprung Display

This marvelous uncaused luminous mind with its miraculous self-sprung unconditioned pristine awareness is a continuous, enjoyable phantasmago-ria. Like space, this display is pure potential, requiring no effort or input or cultivation whatsoever. Even within our bewilderment, pristine awareness emerges instantaneously and adventitiously. The stupor of bewilderment lacking sustained focus or image or concrete idea facilitates pristine awareness because it cannot be crystalized, confined, or obstructed. Bewilderment is thus the basis of the uncaused miracle of momentary display of unimaged illusion. The light ocean of awareness is not the flip side of the dark ocean—it is the dark ocean itself.

Thus even stupidity is suffused by luminous mind. [See also *Pure Golden Ore*, verse 5, and *Great Garuda*, verse 19.]

45

This is the all-inclusive modality
naturally present in all beings;
in the dust storm of blighting delusion
we call for medicine although mind's nature is the cure.[36]

The Equivocating, Doubting Intellect

The notion that all beings, whatever their intelligence, moral status, or state of mind, are included on the path of luminous mind is difficult for the intellect to swallow. Habituated to the distinctions of high and low, pure and impure, intelligent and stupid, and to the idea of a graduated, structured path upon which progress is determined by karma, it is difficult to assimilate the immanence of reality. Even though the rational mind is included in the nondual luminous-mind modality, the immature intellect, left insecure, continues to doubt. Without pure presence we are tainted by delusion and search for an extraneous cure, although the master of medicine is our own mind. We know that buddha is the mind itself, but regardless we continue to look for the solution outside, constantly shifting our focus of search when, inevitably, we fail to find it.

This verse shows that even the slightest motivation to seek the great perfection precludes finding it.

THE TIMELESS MOMENT OF UNIVERSAL ENLIGHTENMENT

46

In the field of ordinary experience lies pure pleasure,
itself the pristine purity of mundane existence;

in every perception finite light is concentrated
and boundless space is established.

The Sublime Retinue

We all know that the nature of mind is buddha and that in the field of pure
presence, buddha is pure pleasure. This understanding accesses the open
dimension of mundane existence.[37] There is no particular object to focus
upon. Indeed, focus, or reification, precludes access to the pure pleasure.
Relaxation into any and all random sensory experience opens up the innate
purity of our ordinary world, an experience concentrated in heightened
awareness and known as light. Our sense organs naturally concentrate the
light of experience while consciousness extends it, filling the ten directions
(the cardinal and intermediate directions, the zenith and nadir) of space,
boundless space, and illuminating it [see verse 50]. Through this simultaneous process of concentration and radiation, all phenomena are experienced
as buddha-deity and luminous mind. Such is the instantaneous process of
enlightenment.

The concentration and radiation of light in the sense organs parallels
the absorption and emergence of light by Samantabhadra in the field of
reality. Whatever he radiates and absorbs is his perfect retinue. His retinue
in pure being (dharmakaya) consists of buddha past, present, and future
and all sentient beings of the sensual, aesthetic, and formless realms and
of the six streams of consciousness. His retinue in the mode of enjoyment
(sambhogakaya) comprises all fleeting emotion and knowledge. His retinue
in the emanation mode (nirmanakaya, or tulku) is the appearances of compassion that are the six kinds of mythic being, the conditioned mind, and
the ocean of activities. His relationship to the retinue, although a unity, is
the same as the relationship of space to the other four great elements, the
relationship of Dzogchen as perfect reality to the 84,000 techniques of
the luminous-mind process, and the relationship of pure essence of mind
to the sensory process.

The concentration of light through awareness may appear to reveal a
method, a yoga of approach, a door into Vajrasattva's reality, and thus constitute a contrived technique; but the process of absorption of light in the
sensory focus and the simultaneous radiation of the light of consciousness
into boundless space is innate and need not be vouchsafed.

This verse and the next show how buddha is revealed in the moment to
everyone.

47

Out of nebulous rainbow light,
the families' distinctive qualities appear;
likewise, as vibrating particles unmoving,
the lord rules the five elements.

The Consummation of Ubhayayoga

In nebulous, amorphous oneness there can be no differentiation of the five families' five distinct colors and qualities. Yet the rainbow light of oneness, like a beam of white light diffracted into a spectrum, is variegated in the mind as five separate colors—white, blue, red, yellow, and green. Within those colors the five buddha families appear with their specific qualities of consciousness. Likewise, without moving one iota, the nature of mind becomes visible in all-inclusive self-sprung awareness. This is Vajrasattva, the overlord of the five elements, and the five elements are fivefold buddha.

Ubhaya, or charyayoga, partakes of both the macrocosmic qualities of kriyayoga and the mental elements of yogatantra. Here the enigma of unity and multiplicity identical is resolved in the reality of Vajrasattva. In this ubhayayoga vision, Vajrasattva is, simultaneously, unitary rainbow light and the efflorescence of the variegated, fivefold colors of the five buddha families out of which the sensory fields manifest. Likewise, he is both the unmoving field out of which the five great vibrating elements arise and the elements themselves that compose the illusory universe. At the center of this mandala of the buddha families, Vajrasattva is the unitary reality. [See also verse 4.]

Thus all beings are already enlightened by Vajrasattva's all-penetrating reality.

THE TIMELESS MOMENT OF GANACHAKRAPUJA

48

"Past," "present," and "future"—
these labels are redundant;
to comprehend what is unborn and unceasing
is to know the sublime unity of time.

Pith Instruction on Notional Time
"Past," "present," and "future" are nominal abstractions. "The past" and "the future" can never exist in the here and now and "the present" exists only as a relational concept. To conceive of past and future is a glitch in the Dzogchen perspective. Past, present, and future never come into existence and never pass into nonexistence: what we have in reality is the sublime unity of time, timelessness, or Great Time. To conceive of and comprehend the three times as uncreated and unceasing is secret instruction on the unity of past, present, and future.

Every moment is a great feast celebration. It is a spontaneous function of the sublime unity of time and space. There is no possibility of temporal structure in luminous-mind reality. Comprehending the unity of time, each moment is complete and perfect in itself. The basis of ritual procedure is thereby undermined, and thereby any and all attachment to the process is eradicated.

The great feast offering (*ganachakrapuja*, or in Tibetan, *tsok cho*) is the central tantric celebration of the nature of reality through sensory indulgence. It is usually performed as a congregational rite. [Verses 48 to 54 relate to aspects of the Dzogchen vision as the great feast offering.]

This verse and the next establish the redundancy of ritual, along with past, present, and future, as fictional mental constructs [see also verse 26].

49

In sameness, temporal creation is impossible;
in oneness, dedication of space is superfluous.
The adorning offerings, naturally arranged,
defy improvement due to intrinsic perfection.

Unequivocal Identity of the Guru and the Offering
Past and future are identical, so the stages of preparation and enactment of offering are the undifferentiated here and now. Through the logic of experiential singularity, the offering (which comprises all phenomena whatsoever), pristine awareness, and the yogin who offers up all phenomena are identical. In this unitary reality, there is no trace of anything concrete anywhere, no reification of offerings, and no distinction between the yogin and the offering. Since there is no dualistic projection, there is nothing to be ritually dedicated. The offerings, adornments of the field of reality, are the five sensual pleasures (sight, sound, taste, smell, and touch), which arise

spontaneously in an arbitrary yet perfect arrangement in natural timeless presence. The absence of any arrangement is itself the perfect arrangement.

Thus pure presence, the donor, and the offering are one in spontaneous giving where dedication and provisional arrangement are redundant.

50

Spontaneity precluding any dedication of the offering,
naturally pure, the universe as offering is already ambrosia;
a specific sense and its consciousness,
in the highest samadhi, are indivisible.

Unequivocal Absence of Motivation in Offering
The offering is always the ornamented field of reality, the totality of the moment. This vast all-inclusive offering is timelessly and spontaneously present, and in its very presence it is made as an offering. Spontaneity precludes the fiction of "dedication," which implies a reification or conceptualization of offering and a projective transference. Besides, the intrinsic perfection of the offering preempts the need for any dedication. Notwithstanding a dualistic perception of the yogin making the offering and the offering itself, since that dichotomy is naturally resolved from the very beginning, the offering is already ambrosia. In the yogin's highest samadhi, the concentrating power of the six senses and the proliferating function of the six consciousnesses [see verse 46] are a unity, and in that perceptual nonduality the blessing is achieved. Any visualization is redundant.

Thus offering is a natural spontaneous function in the here and now.

The Timeless Moment of Spontaneously Perfected Offering of Sensual Pleasure

51

The projecting intellect is the giver,
and the natural arrangement lies in the power of the gaze;
the siddhi inherent in clear seeing
is perfect meditative equipoise.

Making the Universal Offering through the Intellect
In the subtle ritual function of offering, the intellect is the giver, dedicating all phenomena as the offering through a subtle projection of giving into

boundless space. A natural asymmetrical arrangement of the five sensual pleasures (sight, sound, smell, taste, and sensation) is implicit in the sensory gaze.[38] Perceiving the offering as sensorial image, in the clarity or luminosity of the five sensual pleasures lies the siddhi (or realization). In the siddhi resides the samadhi of meditative equipoise. Therein, the accumulation of merit as a causal basis of wish fulfillment and pristine awareness itself are immediately completed.

Thus both the natural function of offering in the moment and the intrinsic spontaneous perfection of ritual offering have been described.

The Timeless Moment of Spontaneity

52

A flash of apprehension is union,
and blissful satisfaction is the commitment;
moving in the dance of skillful means,
nondual union is the offering.

Pith Instruction in Nonunion
Each moment of experience as the nature of mind is a consummate transcendent union. Therein adventitious bliss is the formless commitment (samaya) that is naturally sustained. Within the pure presence of that moment, the field of empty wisdom is momentarily revealed; in the dance of transforming illusion, whatever seeming situation or position arises is an offering in the wholeness of luminous-mind identity. The tantric components of "union," "commitment," "skillful means," and "offering" are defined in terms of nonduality.

In the great perfection of the nature of mind, there is no temporal process wherein two become one because from the beginning there has never been any separation. All is one in luminous mind. So "union" is a recognition of the inexpressible nature of luminous mind, wherein pure pleasure is always the feeling tone. Although in anuyuga, luminous mind is defined in terms of the union of pure presence and the field of reality,[39] still that union is never consummated and never cloven and the skillful dance is a constant offering.

Thus the great feast rite is momentary spontaneity.

THE TIMELESS MOMENT OF INFINITE RITUAL

53

Detached generosity is the torma,
and nonaction instantaneously consummates ritual;
unthought pristine awareness dissolves obstacles,
and unspoken meditative equipoise is the hymn of praise.

The Consummation of Ritual Performance

Each moment is a spontaneous nonritual torma offering. In pure presence
the phenomenal world is utterly forsaken without a shred of grasping, clinging—or even apprehension. In the space of complete sameness, no action is
superior to any other. But when the ritual of torma offering, for example, is
performed, perceptual nonduality is represented by the torma (generally a
cone-shaped parched barley cake, laced with molasses, decorated with symbols of transcendence to represent aspects of buddha mind). Nondirected
action transcends the yogin's performance of the ritual, which is therefore
consummated before it is done. Here unthinking pristine awareness is the
Lord of the Directions; here the Lord of Obstructing Forces immediately
dissolves subtle obstacles and thought forms[40] created by the offering ritual;
and here nonverbal meditative equipoise is the Lord of Uncontrived Activity,
Lord of Nonaction, who sings the hymns of praise. In this way the elements
of ritual naturally express the spontaneous moment-to-moment luminous-
mind modality and the ritual performance of kriyayoga—vajra-kriya—is
perfected by the transcendent nature of mind.

THE TIMELESS MOMENT OF THE GREAT BIND: THE CHAINS OF SELF-IMPORTANT GIVING

54

Veneration of the lama, generosity,
and all such meritorious activity
become a serious bind
when enacted without imperturbable detachment.

The Glitch of Goal-Directed Action

In the modality of the great perfection, it is not the nature of the action
but the attitude that counts, and bad attitude is disclosed in attachment to

a goal or attention to the result of an action. Even if the result is the virtue that serves one's own or another's purpose, like moral conduct and patience, goal orientation puts the mind into a dualistic frame and binds it. Worshiping the guru-lama with offerings given for the purpose of receiving blessing or some mundane benefit, or giving alms to beggars or gifts to friends with an ulterior motive, is a glitch in the luminous-mind process unless it is performed with the complete indifference provided by an immovable samadhi of desirelessness.

This glitch in behavior—which may by extension apply to any activity wherein attachment lies—is stressed as a terrible bind, not so much as through the self-involvement inherent in the act but through goal-directed motivation. Without the samadhi of sameness we are caught in a double bind. We are wrong if we do not worship the teacher; we are wrong if we venerate him with regular attachment. It is imperative to make offering, but only without attachment. In the praxis of the Great Perfection, however, the great bind is reflexively released. Come what may, the nature of the moment is spontaneously resolved.

Thus we gain release from lama worship.

THE TIMELESS MOMENT OF SYMBOLIC TRANSMISSION

55

**About this very transmission,
if it is structured it becomes a veil;
if conceptualized, similarly,
its reality can never be achieved.**

Seminal Instruction on this Great Transmission

If we search for literal meaning, we are bound by it and lose it. If we strive for effortlessness we cannot find it. So in this transmission of total perfection, if effortless nonseeking turns into striving, we are diseased and veiled. If, however, we realize nonaction here and now, reality can never become concrete.

The purpose of this transmission is to resolve all experience whatsoever in complete perfection. Inasmuch as the experience of the transmission consists of comprehension of its heart meaning, its purpose is to deconstruct and dissolve the veils that hide its reality. Thus to structure its content in any way is to defy its purpose. To conceptualize its meaning or to turn it into a religious practice or a yoga is also to defeat its purpose. Ambiguity is an intrinsic element of its dynamic. Insofar as we seek solid literal meanings, its internal dialectic is frustrated.

Thus we are cautioned that the words of the transmission are the finger pointing at the moon and not the moon itself.

NOTES

See appendix 1 for abbreviations used in the notes.

1 See Patrul Rimpoche, "The Three Incisive Precepts" (Dowman 2003, 181).
2 Vairotsana first received from Shri Singha the eighteen Mind Series transmissions, which included his own Five Early Translations (*snga 'gyur lnga*) and thirteen transmissions translated later by Vimalamitra, and then the Matrix Series transmissions.
3 This account of Vairotsana is derived from various, sometimes conflicting, sources. One significant variation is the location of Vairotsana's encounter with Shri Singha, which is given as Vajrasana (Bodh Gaya) in some sources, most particularly in the *Bairo 'dra 'bag*, the canonial hagiography of Vairotsana (see Yudra Nyingpo 2004, *The Great Image: The Life Story of Vairochana*). But "Vajrasana" may be understood figuratively as the seat of all enlightenment. See also Norbu and Clemente 1999, 46–56.
4 The six lines of the *Cuckoo's Song (Rig pa'i khu byug)* are called *The Six Vajra Verses (Rdo rje tshig drug)* in the *Supreme Source*, where they are said to define the nature of Samantabhadra himself as spontaneously complete and perfect nonaction. The *Ten Sutras* commentary takes the verses to be a transmission of the precept of undiscriminating enjoyment.
5 The *Supreme Source (Kun byed rgyal po)* introduces *Radical Creativity (Rtsal chen sprugs pa)* like this: "This great transmission is Samantabhadra's inspired precept and reveals the free-form immaculate field of reality (basic spaciousness) as the field of his radical creativity, which is nonaction."
6 The *Great Garuda in Flight (Khyung chen lding ba)* should not be confused with Shri Singha's work or any of several others with similar titles. The *Ten Sutras* commentary distinguishes between a first part (verse 1–16) that constitutes specific instruction, primarily on nonmeditation, and a second part (verses 17–26) that treats various aspects of the yogin's career.
7 *Sems nyid rang snang gi rnam pa las / stong pa 'gyur ba med pa'i dbyings shes bar byas.* (*Gnas lugs mdzod 'grel ba*, p. 84, fol. 35. In Dowman 2009, canto 71: "Any aspect of the gestalt imagery of the nature of mind should be known as the spaciousness that is unchangeable emptiness."
8 This "particle" or "nucleus" (*rdul phran gcig*) is at once a subatomic particle that cannot be divided and the sole seminal seed of totality (*thig le nyag cig*). There are variant readings for *gses shing*.

9   "Sacred and profane" renders "Dharma and non-Dharma" (*chos dang chos min*).

10   "Sages" (*drang srong*) can refer to Indian rishis or to Bon monks.

11   See Norbu and Clemente 1999, 280n205, for Longchenpa's commentary on these first eleven verses.

12   This ambiguous line may also be read as "all are free from conventional morality" or "all have abandoned worldly sin" (*kha na ma tho 'jig rten spong*). See also Dowman 2009, canto 122ii, p. 247.

13   See also *Pure Golden Ore*, verse 8, below. The following seven lines have been removed from the body of translation because they seem to be an irrelevant interpolation breaking the flow of meaning (the *Ten Sutras* has no commentary on these lines). Perhaps they were added due to the strong force of their argument urging nonaction, which is the topic of this particular transmission. "Because all experience is in the present, / the nature of experience is the here and now; / so the phenomenal mind seeking itself, / space seeking the nature of space / as if reality were something extraneous, / is like trying to extinguish fire with fire, / and that is a very difficult task." The intellect cannot see or isolate its own nature, and in the effort and striving to objectify itself, it creates a stream of discursive analytic thought together with misguided ideas about how to achieve consummation that merely muddy the water further. Conversely trying to stop thinking merely creates further thought and is like adding fire to fire.

14   The title *Pure Golden Ore* (*Rdo la gser zhun*) provides a metaphor for the intrinsic purity of our every experience. Suffused by gold, ore is no less precious than purified gold itself. The gentle youth, or gentle virgin prince, who personifies the luminous mind that suffuses all experience, is Manjushri Kumara ('*Jam dpal gzhon nu*), known more conventionally as the bodhisattva of intelligence and the protector of mind. Identified with the pure essence of mind, the fount of all and everything, he is omniscient.

15   The text has *lo rgyus don gnyis*, which may be taken to indicate both its absolute (*rang don*) and specific (*spyi don*) meaning. The *Ten Sutras* treats history (*lo rgyus*) under three headings: blessing (*byin brlabs*), "own essence" (*rang gi ngo bo*), and scripture (*tshig sdebs*).

16   The *three mahayoga samadhis* are taken as the here-and-now samadhi (*de bzhin nyid kyi ting nge 'dzin*), the all-illuminating samadhi (*kun tu snang gi ting nge 'dzin*), and the seed-syllable samadhi (*rgyu'i ting nge 'dzin*) and relate respectively to the three dimensions of essence, nature, and compassion.

17   These twelve lines appended to *Pure Golden Ore* appear to be a later insertion. The *Ten Sutras* adds this concluding verse: "The all-transcending six nuclei, / immune to any inflation or deflation, / by dint of their unborn and unceasing nature / reveal the meaning of nonmeditation." The *six nuclei* are the nucleus of reality (*chos nyid kyi thig le*), the nucleus of basic spaciousness (*dbyings kyi thig le*), the nucleus of the utterly pure spaciousness (*dbyings rnam par dag pa'i thig le*), the nucleus of pristine awareness (*ye shes chen pa'i thig le*), the nucleus of Samantabhadra (*kun tu bzang pa'i thig le*), and the nucleus of spontaneity (*lhun gyi grub pa'i thig le*). It may be relevant to note that some sources include the *Six Seminal Nuclei* (*Thig le drug pa*) among the Five Early Translations.

18   Also known as *The Vast Space of Vajrasattva* (*Rdo rje sems dpa' nam mkha' che*), *The Eternal Victory Banner* or *The Ever-Unfurled Victory Banner* (*Mi nub rgyal mtshan*) is introduced in the Collected Tantras of Vairotsana as the root of all pith instruction and transmission. In the *Supreme Source* Samantabhadra introduces the transmission like this: "Listen, Sempa Dorje, / I will show you, Sempa Dorje, / your own nature. / I, the

supreme source, I am your nature / and I am timeless luminous mind / and luminous mind is like this."

19 The third sutra of the *Ten Sutras* addresses the first three parts of the fivefold excellence of the teacher, the teaching, his retinue, the place, and the time. The nature of the perfect teacher, Samantabhadra, is demonstrated here (verse 1); the excellent teaching is luminous mind (verse 41 and also 42); the nature of the excellent retinue is the three modes of being within pure presence (verse 46). The excellent place is the vast spaciousness of the field of reality treated in verses 16 and 9; and the excellent time is the unity of time treated in verses 26 and 48.

20 The fifth sutra of the *Ten Sutras* treats the five exaltations (*che ba rnam lnga*): the exaltation of enlightenment here and now (*mngon par sangs rgyas che*) expressed as the fivefold excellence (see note 19 above), exaltation of the enlightened field of reality (verse 16), exaltation of enlightened identity (verse 33), exaltation of the evidence of enlightenment (verse 40), and exaltation of nonenlightenment (verse 8).

21 The seventh sutra of the *Ten Sutras* treats the three kinds of transmission: direct transmission, or emanation in the nature of mind (verse 19); the aural transmission (verse 22); and transmission ultimately resolving all experience (verse 3).

22 Verses 4, 5, and 6 show the intrinsic perfection of the nature of mind regardless of meditation technique. In the ninth chapter of the *Ten Sutras*, the commentary upon these verses shows how mahayoga, anuyoga, and sattvayoga (verses 4, 5, and 6, respectively), subsumed by Dzogchen, facilitate realization of this perfection.

23 TB has "reality" (*chos nyid*, Skt. *dharmata*); BGB has "teaching" or "dharma" (*chos 'di*).

24 The seventh sutra of the *Ten Sutras* also addresses pith instruction (*man ngag*, alternatively translated as "secret precept") on luminous mind (verse 9); on nonunion (verse 52); on notional time (verse 48); and on seminal instruction on this great transmission (verse 55). See Dowman 2009, canto 84, p. 189, for the master's comment upon the status of karma presented in verses 9 and 10.

25 The sixth sutra of the *Ten Sutras* treats glitches and veils in a sixfold enumeration: (1) the glitch of belief in progress on a path (verse 21); (2) the glitch of striving (verse 20); (3) the glitch of goal-directed action (verse 54); (4) the glitch of moral discrimination (verse 14); (5) the glitch of subtle method (verse 13); and (6) the glitch of concentrated absorption (verse 12).

26 Consider the mahayoga completion stage (*rdzogs rim*) precepts of physical, verbal, and mental solitude (*lus sngags sems dben*).

27 The eighth sutra of the *Ten Sutras* treats the five certainties and three equivocations: (1) the unequivocal unity of time (verse 26), (2) the unequivocal identity of the guru and the offering (verse 49), (3) the unequivocal absence of motivation in offering (verse 50), (4) the unequivocal absence of indication of attainment (verse 43), and (5) the unequivocal congruence of pleasure and pain (verse 15); along with (6) the equivocal nature of experience (verse 35); (7) the equivocating, doubting intellect (verse 45); and (8) the unpredictable pristine awareness (verse 25).

28 The fourth sutra of the *Ten Sutras* treats the four yogas: the reality of Dzogchen atiyoga (verse 42), the reality of Dzogchen anuyoga (verse 17), the reality of creative mahayoga (verse 37), and the reality of tantrayoga (verse 36). See *Great Garuda*, verse 1, where the concept of the dharmakaya is equated with the dharmakaya itself, and verses 49 and 50 below, where the reality of anuyoga is trumped by spontaneity.

29 Verses 18 and 19 treat reality in terms of language. A dharani (an extensive, elaborate concatenation of syllables), which is the mudra, is a formulation of gnosemes (particles

of sound or vibration): such "unions" of vowels and consonants describe a seemingly concrete reality, yet as emanations of dharmakaya their reality is empty buddha speech. In union with the dharani (the mudra) there is no distinction between the gnosemic or verbal formulation and the great display of Samantabhadra. (But see verse 52 on nonunion.)

30 TB has *ma bral smon pas spyod pas na*; BGB *ma bral smon pa spyod pas na*; and DC supports this with *chags dang ma bral*. NCG has *bya bral smon pa spyod pas na* and thus inverts the meaning: "action unmotivated in time / this is 'empty action'"; where conduct is unmotivated, that activity is said to be "empty."

31 The word *tha tshigs* in the first and last lines of the verse may be rendered as either a synonym of *tha snyad*, "conventional designation," or as *dam tshig* (Skt. *samaya*), "commitment." The *Ten Sutras* takes the first interpretation.

32 BGB has *A dang par ni rnam ldan na*, while the *Ten Sutras* has *Lung gi a dang ston pa'i sar ldan na*: "endowed with the *a* of the transmission on the level of the teacher." See NCG, chapters 7 and 8.

33 This line (*snang 'dod rtsol sems bde ba la*) from TB is glossed in the *Ten Sutras* by "hankering after appearances" (*snang bar 'dod cing rtsol sems byed pa*), which is the obscuration. See also *Great Garuda*, verse 15, regarding this verse.

34 See Norbu and Clemente 1999, 172, and Dowman 2009, canto 115, p. 231, which has a line interpolated between the third and fourth lines: "that is nondual knowledge and ignorance."

35 Rongzom (see Clemente 1999, 55n9) has "contaminated" (*bslad*) instead of "easy" (*sla*): the natural state is veiled by contaminating concepts. The phrase "unequivocal absence of any indication of attainment" (*dka' sla mtshon du med pa*) that heads the commentary is an inadequate rendering of the notion that it is impossible to say whether access to luminous mind is easy or difficult, or whether indeed there is any access at all.

36 BGB has "we innocents, because of tainting delusion / are like medicine seeking a doctor" (*byis pas 'khrul pas bslad pa'i phyir / sman nyid sman pa 'tshol ba bzhin*). TB has *bus pas bslad bas 'khrul pa'i phyir.*

37 On the progressive paths, understanding (*go ba*), experiencing (*nyams pa*), and realization (*rtogs pa*) are three stages of increasing assimilation of knowledge to the intellect. In this Dzogchen analysis, within mere comprehension (*go ba*), or within every fleeting thought or concept (*rtog pa*), lies realization (*togs pa*).

38 In the third line of the verse (in the second line of the translation), TB has "the offering that is seen" (*bltas ba'i tshogs ni*) rather than "the power of the gaze" (*bltas ba'i stobs*), as it is in BGB and *Ten Sutras*.

39 In anuyoga, the union of pure presence (*rig pa*) and the field of reality (*dbyings*) is represented by the union of father-buddha Samantabhadra and mother-buddha Samantabhadri. On union, see also verses 5, 18, and 32.

40 Obstacles to meditation may be personified as spirits called *geks* (*'gegs*).

Appendix 4
The Tibetan Texts and Commentaries

The following abbreviations are used here and in the annotation:

BGB   Collected Tantras of Vairotsana. *Bairo rgyud 'bum*, 8 vols. Leh: S. W. Tashigangpa, 1971.

TB   Collected Tantras of the Ancients. *Rnying ma rgyud 'bum*, Mtshams brag edition, 46 vols. Thimphu, Bhutan: National Library, Royal Government of Bhutan, 1982. See also online at the University of Virginia: http://www.thlib.org/encyclopedias/literary/canons/ngb/catalog.php#cat=ng

NCG *The Tantra of the Vast Space of Vajrasattva. Rdo rje sems dpa' nam mkha' che'i rgyud.* TB vol. *ga*, 165.3–191.

KG   *Supreme Source. Kun byed rgyal po. Kulayarāja.* TB vol. *ka*, 1–288.

DC   *Ten Sutras. Mdo bcu (The Sutra that Includes All Experience within the Luminous Mind of the Great Perfection. Chos thams cad rdzogs pa chen po byang chub kyi sems su 'dus pa'i mdo).* TB vol. *ka*, 352–499.

The Five Early Translations appear in the Collected Tantras of Vairotsana (BGB) and as chapters of the *Supreme Source* (KG). They are also quoted in the *Ten Sutras* (DC) in the context of their commentary. The BGB is the oldest but most corrupt. My commentary to the transmissions is derived primarily from the explanatory text the *Ten Sutras*, the second text in the Collected Tantras of the Ancients (TB), (the second text in the "atiyoga section"). Of the various tantras in TB with *Rdo rje sems dpa' nam mkha' che* in the title, the *Tantra of the Vast Space of Vajrasattva (Rdo rje sems dpa' nam mkha' che' i rgyud)* and, likewise, its *Lcags 'grel* commentary (BGB vol. *nga*, 397–453) has sometimes shed light on verses in *Eternal Victory Banner*.

The following verses or lines are quoted by Longchenpa in *Byang chub kyi sems kun byed rgyal po'i don khrid rin chen sgru bo*, translated in the book *You Are the Eyes of the World* (Longchenpa 1987): *Radical Creativity*, verse 6 on pp. 24–25; *Pure Golden Ore*, verse 7 in note 42; *Eternal Victory Banner*, verse 16 on p. 40 and verse 40 on p. 43.

The following verses or lines are quoted by Longchenpa in *Gnas lugs mdzod 'grel ba*, which I translated in *Natural Perfection* (Dowman 2009): *Eternal Victory Banner*, verses 9 and 10 in canto 84, p. 189; the first couplet of verse 30 in canto 85, p. 191, and in canto 113, p. 228; and verses 41, 42, and 44 in parts in canto 115, p. 231. *Great Garuda* verses 2–4 are quoted in part in canto 8, pp. 71–72; verse 10 in canto 33, p. 121; verse 12 in part in canto 63, p.158; verse 14 in canto 12, p. 228; and verse 21 in part in canto 125, p. 242.

SOURCES OF THE FIVE EARLY TRANSLATIONS AND ALTERNATE ENGLISH TRANSLATIONS

The Cuckoo's Song of Pure Presence (Rig pa'i khu byug)
   IOL/Stein 647 in the Tun Huang (Dunhuang) collection.
   TB vol. *ka*, 113.2–5; KG, chap. 31.
   TB vol. *ka*, 453.3–6; DC, in the eighth sutra.
   BGB vol. *nga*, 306.

   Karmay 2007, 50.
   Reynolds 1996, 232–33.
   Norbu and Shane 1986, xv.
   Norbu and Clemente 1989, 48.
   Norbu and Clemente 1999, 174.

Radical Creativity (Rtsal chen sprugs pa)
   TB vol. *ka*, 98.7–100.1; KG, chap. 27.
   TB vol. *ka*, 453.6–455.1; DC, in the eighth sutra.
   BGB vol. *nga*, 306–8.

   Norbu and Clemente 1999, 165.
   J. Valby 2011, 2:36

Great Garuda in Flight (Khyung chen lding ba)
  TB vol. *ka*, 87.2–91.6; KG, chap. 22.
  TB vol. *ka*, 455.1–462.4; DC, in the eighth sutra.
  BGB vol. *nga*, 308–14.

  Norbu and Clemente 1999, 158–61.
  J. Valby 2011, 2:26–29.

Pure Golden Ore (Rdo la gser zhun)
  TB vol. *ka*, 96.4–98.6; KG, chap. 26.
  TB vol. *ka*, 450.3–453.3; DC, in the eighth sutra.

  Norbu and Clemente 1999, 163–65.

Eternal Victory Banner: The Vast Space of Vajrasattva (Mi nub pa'i rgyal mtshan: Nam mkha' che)
  TB vol. *ka*, 105.2–113.1; KG, chap. 30.
  TB vol. *ka*, 352–499; in the tenth sutras of the DC.
  BGB vol. *nga*, 383–95.

  Clemente 1999.
  Norbu and Clemente 1999, 168–73.
  Valby 2011, 1:4–10.

ༀ

Appendix 2
Mind Series Terminology

The following abbreviations are employed as indices in the subsequent analysis: CS = Cuckoo's Song; RC = Radical Creativity; GG = Great Garuda; PG = Pure Golden Ore; and VB = Eternal Victory Banner. The "c" denotes citation from the respective commentary.

Dzogchen texts are divided into three series or classes: Mind Series (*sems sde*), Matrix (or Vast Expanse) Series (*klong sde*), and Secret Precept Series (*man ngag sde*). The Five Early Translations are seminal texts of the Mind Series, and the *Supreme Source* (*Kun byed rgyal po*) contains all the principal Mind Series texts. The simplest explanation for the existence of three separate series is three distinct geographical sources of the tradition. Scant evidence exists in support of this hypothesis but a comparative examination of terminology would seem to encourage it. Certainly the vocabulary of the transmissions helps to confirm these Mind Series texts as the earliest Dzogchen scriptures. Dzogchen terminology was still evidently in an incipient phase and had not developed into the lexicon of later exegesis. It was as if Vairotsana were employing a vernacular expression to translate his experience, very much as we struggle to translate the Tibetan into English. The language of the *Ten Sutras* on the other hand is written with a more highly developed Dzogchen lexicon and argues for a much later date of composition by an author other than Vairotsana. In the transmissions, for example, the words "reality" (*chos nyid*) and, surprisingly, "pure presence" (*rig pa*) rarely appear, and likewise "basic spaciousness of the field of reality" (dharmadhatu) and "pure being" (dharmakaya). The word "matrix" or "expanse" (*klong*), a vital notion in elaborated Dzogchen, does not appear in the transmissions and only once in the commentary. The term "ground of being" (*kun gzhi*, Skt. *alaya*) does not appear (although see PG2). The phrase "nondual perception" (*gzung 'dzin med pa*) does not appear in the transmissions, although it does frequently in the *Ten Sutras* commentary. The term "seminal nucleus" or "all-inclusive nucleus" (*thig le chen po*) appears once in the transmissions (PG10), although the notion of the "one indivisible particle" (*rdul phran gcig*) (GG3) seems to mean the same thing. Predictably, "emptiness" (*stong pa nyid*), a favorite term of the dialecticians, does not appear in the transmissions, although the commentary uses it occasionally.

Further, the transmissions do not mention the three dimensions of being (*trikaya*) while the commentary stresses the unity of the three as the one dharmakaya. Nor are the four yogas or the nine approaches mentioned, although one of the main themes of the *Ten Sutras* is the assimilation of the gradual approaches into radical Dzogchen. The commentary to *Eternal Victory Banner* verses 4, 5, and 6 applies the natural modality of the Great Perfection to mahayoga, anuyoga, and outer yogatantra (sattvayoga), where each is shown as complete and perfect. This is in contradistinction to the commentary to verses 17, 27, 36, and 42 upon the reality of anuyoga, maha-yoga, tantrayoga, and atiyoga respectively, where anuyoga is described as a "subtle technique" while mahayoga and tantrayoga are considered incomplete. The absence of these and other enumerations and conceptual frames in the transmissions argues a very early date and very pure antecedents for the Mind Series transmissions of radical Dzogchen.

Basic spaciousness that is the field of reality, basic spaciousness, field of reality, reality-field, etc. (*chos dbyings*, *dharmadhatu*)

The first distinction to be made in the temporal development of consciousness in childhood is between inside and outside, subject and object. The tendency to concretize self and other dominates our ordinary perception, but true reality is a unified field of experience that viewed holistically is called the dharmadhatu, which is rendered herein as "basic spaciousness." The first three verses of *Radical Creativity* describe it as Samantabhadra's emanation, which is our own field of experience. It is a unitary field super-seding all outer and inner distinctions and time itself (VB26). It is a field of ultimate identity and equality. It is perfect in itself, unalterable and immovable. It is a dynamic field of experience free of any directed activity, and thus it can be described as a "free-form display" (RCc3). In the first two verses of *Great Garuda*, Samantabhadra's emanation as basic spaciousness is shown "individuated" as the mind of the Dzogchen yogin and therefore as the Dzogchen modality, in which a field, as luminous mind, cannot be anywhere located, a non-field in perceptual nonduality, nondiscursive and nonanalytical. Although it is "individuated," the dharmadhatu is still unlimited, uncircumscribed, without center or circumference (GG5).

If Samantabhadra is the nondual wholeness of being and knowing, Vajrasattva is the vast spaciousness of the field of reality within pure being, or "individuated emptiness" (VB1). The field of reality is thus the space in which all and everything agglomerates and is reflexively released as Vajrasattva in a constant unimpeded process. *Dharmadhatu* may be rendered simply as "spaciousness" or as "existential space."

In the anuyoga view, basic spaciousness is posited as the complement of pure presence (*rig pa*) in a union of the gender principles of skillful means and insight. Thus the Dzogchen unity of the single Samantabhadra is provisionally split to show Samantabhadra as pure presence in union with Samantabhadri as reality itself (VB5).

The five passions arise in luminous mind, and the five sensual pleasures are described as "ornaments" of the spaciousness of the field of reality. As such they partake of the nature of reality and therefore can have no appearance, no form, no shape, and no color (VB16). In the same way, the universe as an offering of sensual pleasure is described in terms of an "adornment" of basic spaciousness, so the offering is an offering of basic spaciousness as emptiness (VB49).

Body, speech, and mind (*sku gsung thugs*)
The three dimensions of body, speech, and mind are one in luminous mind and one in pure being. The elaboration of the fundamental unity into three aspects provides a skillful means of illuminating the delusive miasmas of the six kinds of mythic being in three dimensions. Human "body," "speech," and "mind" refer to the dimensions of structured emanational being, of energy flows and patterns, and of consciousness, respectively. Buddha "body," "speech," and "mind" refer to the natural sameness of those dimensions in luminous mind. Buddha body, speech, and mind are like the eyes of luminous mind that recognize the variety of beings, the passions, the suffering, and the sensual pleasures on the wheel of life, as luminous mind. More specifically, buddha body, speech, and mind are the purity of the three poisons in luminous mind: buddha body, recognizing the tendency to attraction

and desire and its manifestations; buddha speech, recognizing the tendency to aversion and anger; and buddha mind, recognizing all forms of bewilderment and ignorance. In conceptual meditation the centers of body, speech, and mind are located in the head, throat, and heart respectively.

Buddha (*sang rgyas pa*)

In the radical Dzogchen view there are no separate entities called "buddhas." Rather, there is *buddha*, which is synonymous with enlightenment (nonenlightenment). Further, the anglicization *buddhahood* enlarges the gap between realization and the here and now, so simply "buddha" is preferred herein. Buddha refers to the ineffable reality of nondual experience, which cannot be dualized in any way.

Field, object (*yul*)

In the delusive dualistic analysis of perception, objects of the senses—the objective field—are grasped by consciousness, "the knower." In nondual perception there is no object to grasp, and the sensory fields are basic spaciousness: the field of reality, the dharmadhatu.

Luminous mind (*byang chub sems, bodhichitta*)

There is a strong case for assimilating the word *bodhichitta*, by which we understand compassionate buddha mind, into the English language—we possess no equivalent. "Enlightened mind" or "awakened mind" is the phrase most commonly employed as equivalent in the Vajrayana. But in the Vajrayana enlightened mind is the prerogative of buddha only, whereas in Dzogchen it is the very stuff of all-embracing reality. Bodhichitta is reality itself—"luminous mind and reality are one in basic spaciousness" (RCc1–2), as mind and inner space are one (GGc1). The nondual imperative of Dzogchen requires a more neutral, less affective equivalent for bodhichitta, and for that reason I have chosen *luminous mind*, the luminous mind that supersedes or transcends the rational mind without any sense of moral quality. Luminous mind is also the sole recourse of beings trapped on a causal path, because it is the one cause and the sole effect (GGc1). Luminous mind, however, is also identified as loving-kindness (VB2) and selfless compassion (GGc14). Since the term defines the Mind Series of Dzogchen precepts, its meaning is paramount and justifies its dominant incidence in the texts.

Nature of mind (*sems nyid*)

The seminal phrase the "nature of mind" does not appear in the transmissions. Luminous mind and the pure essence of mind are the nature of mind and subsume all its meanings.

Nonaction; adj. free-form (*bya med*; *bya bral*)

"Nonaction" may imply the unmoving nature of basic spaciousness (GG1), the dharmadhatu itself (GGc1), but it is, simultaneously, the play of sameness or emptiness in multiplicity, and for that reason sometimes herein it has been rendered "free-form," like the sky. Nonaction is nondirected action or spontaneous, free-form action (RC3); it is spontaneity itself. It is the yogi's activity that is an integral part of the dynamic, miraculous display of Samantabhadra (GG24). There is no self-directed motivation, and indeed there is no motivation whatsoever. There is no effort involved, no goal-oriented striving, no seeking for the sake of finding (VBc55). There is no connotation of "hard work" or "onerous duty." It may imply renunciation of all mundane involvement, but not necessarily so. It may imply the abandonment of all spiritual materialism, including meditation, devotional exercises, and ritual, but again not necessarily so (VB21). This definition is inclining toward "nonaction" as an attitude to the dynamic of body, speech, and mind (VB53). With this attitude the spectacular display of appearances, including the yogin, is a constant, but nothing is ever done. At the same time everything is released (VB3).

The Five Early Translations belong to those chapters of the *Supreme Source* that treat perfected nonaction. But the word appears only rarely therein and rarely in the *Ten Sutras* commentary. Its significance, however, is seminal in Dzogchen exegesis.

Path, process, modality (*lam*)

If a path implies a distinct starting point, a temporal progression, and a destination, Maha Ati has no path—or it is better designated a pathless path, the path always under our feet that has no extension. And yet within a timeless moment of luminous mind, there is an unfoldment and a release. For this reason "path" has sometimes been rendered as "process." To emphasize the synchronistic function of "arising," "abiding," and "releasing," "modality" has frequently been preferred to "path" or "process."

Pristine awareness (*ye shes, jnana*)

This basic awareness is forever fresh, never becoming tired, bored, or jaded. There is an element of the ingenuousness of the simpleton in it since it cannot be elaborated into a complex proposition. Since it is nondual perception, nothing can transcend it and it cannot be objectified; it can therefore be rendered as "ultimate awareness." Since it exists as original reality, it can be rendered as "primordial awareness." It has no cause or condition and arises spontaneously by and of itself and it is thus "self-sprung awareness." Direct perception and nondual cognition are pristine awareness in basic spaciousness that is all luminous mind; it is spontaneous, instantaneous cognition. It cannot be discovered by seeking (VBc20) and it is immune to contextualization (VBc25). It arises in an unimpeded samadhi (VBc1), imperturbable (VB32). Nothing can induce it or develop it. The modality of release is inherent within it (VB3). Its nature is natural pure pleasure (VBc26). Pure presence is a function of pristine awareness (VB42).

Thought itself is pristine awareness because the dharmakaya as a concept is naturally indeterminate and pure (GG1). Thought in itself is thought-free, and pristine awareness is "a ubiquitous, unthinking, authentic presence" (GG1). It has no location, no specifics, and it is noncomposite (GGc3). It transcends all thought and expression, absorbing all specific meaning into one single sovereign sameness. The basic spaciousness that is the field of reality is spontaneously and constantly suffused by pristine awareness. Pristine awareness is a wish-fulfilling jewel (GG12). Pristine awareness is the eye of direct insight, the eye of omniscience, that sees the spacious nature of the field of reality (PG6).

Although it cannot be located, it can be recognized in the natural union of means and insight (anuyoga) (VB5). Desire, anger, and bewilderment arise as pristine awareness (VB16). Pristine awareness arises particularly in the state of bewilderment as Samantabhadra's miraculous display (VB44). It spontaneously arises in thought (VB12), in the spaciousness of mental constructs (anuyoga) (VB17). In the perspective of sattvayoga, the buddha-deity of pristine awareness identifies with the yogi. In ubhayayoga vision, pristine awareness is radiated from the nature of mind as Vajrasattva, who is inseparable from the five colors and the five elements (VBc47). The offering of the sensual pleasures, the individuated mind that is making the offering, and pristine awareness are all one within the offering ritual (VBc49).

Bewilderment (*gti mug*), or a state of stupidity, is clouded pristine awareness that possesses the same undiscriminating facility as pristine awareness itself, and therefore pristine awareness arises easily within it, or rather it is timelessly inherent in it, and spontaneously emerges therein (PG5). The scriptures themselves and momentary visions appear in misty awareness (GG19).

Pure being (*chos sku, dharmakaya*)

If *dharmadhatu* refers to the holistic experiential field of spaciousness, *dharmakaya* refers to the ontic dimension of the totality, to pure being itself. The word "being" in English, within its abstract, common meaning realized by all sentient life, has a personalized sense that allows the notion of buddha in human form. This limitation, however, is belied by its definition as "unthought sameness" (VB18), which is a close synonym of "emptiness," a term seldom used in Dzogchen exegesis. "The reality of luminous mind is like space; mind, unthinking and without constructs, is the sameness of pure being" (VBc18). Within pure being, luminous-mind reality lacks any concrete name or form whatsoever—it is utterly insubstantial—so there is nothing to grasp and hold on to. Within the unoriginated dharmakaya of Samantabhadra, the magical illusion of creation becomes apparent, and all of creation is Samantabhadra's display.

Within pure being, magical illusion arises composed of the five aggregates, which as secondary emanations of the eight consciousnesses comprise the complete sphere of activity of the threefold mundane finite world, a world that takes the form of the five passions' five sensory pleasures (VBc19). In this sense, pure being is all-inclusive. But since luminous mind never becomes any thing, never becomes any shape, size, or color, and therefore, insofar as it never moves out of its own nature, it is immovable and unchangeable (VBc32); known as pure being, present as the stance (mudra) of pure being; and as a seal of pure being, it is free of perceptual duality. The self-sprung awareness of pure being remains constant in an imperturbable samadhi. So pure being is pristine awareness.

In *Great Garuda* (verses 1–3) a distinction is made between the notional dharmakaya that is the object of goal-oriented meditation and pure being that is pristine awareness. The notional dharmakaya as a concept refers to nothing at all and therefore, simultaneous with its conception, self-sprung awareness arises. The same may be said for any concept whatsoever, so all thought is pure being.

Pure being and pristine awareness (*sku dang ye shes*)

Luminous mind has no structure, yet it is described didactically in terms of being (*sku*) and awareness (*ye shes*), a putative dualism of its ontic and epistemic aspects (VBc6). "Pure being" refers to the structure of reality, though since this structure has no concrete reality and no temporal or spatial limitations, perhaps "antistructure" is more meaningful. It could be described as the unidimensional reality of luminous mind, since it is not elaborated in time or space, yet it appears as variegated multiplicity. This structure may be differentiated as the three modes of pure being—dharmakaya, sambhogakaya, and nirmanakaya—but such a distinction is mentioned only once in the five transmissions and that in the commentary. Pristine awareness is the all-inclusive pure cognition of buddha. So pure being is luminous mind, and pristine awareness is its innate propensity for cognition. As a skillful means, realization of the unity of the ontic (*sku*) and epistemic (*ye shes*) voids the appearance of substantiality in the sensory fields by facilitating the union of subject and object. They are united as a union of "the immovable" and "the imperturbable" (VBc32).

The all-inclusive magical illusion of luminous mind is actualized by an involuntary realization of its unitary nature of "suchness." Then it can be described as indivisible "pure being" in its ontic reality and "pristine awareness" in its epistemic aspect (VBc6). Likewise, in realization of the wheel of life as the modality of luminous mind, the phantasmagoric display is a union of pure being and the five aspects of pristine awareness (VB9c). Again, insofar as the field of buddha experience is devoid of perceptual duality—any structure based on consciousness, sense organ, and sensory object, the fictions of dualistic analysis—buddha experience in pure being is described in terms of pure being and pristine awareness (VBc16).

Pure essence of mind (*byang chub snying po, bodhigarbha*)

As the one and only cause, luminous mind is the pure essence of mind, the source of all things (VBc33). "Essence" is here a rendering of *snying po*, which can also be translated as "womb," "matrix," or "heart." However, "essence" is to be understood as emptiness, never as even the most-subtle concrete quintessence. Since luminous mind is free of any substantial *ens* or self, the connotation of substance is always inappropriate. The physical image of the word "womb" makes it inappropriate as an equivalent of *snying po* in the Dzogchen context because it implies a separation of the container and the contents. The pure essence of mind is bodhichitta as the sole cause, not to be separated from bodhichitta as the sole effect. The essence and the manifestation are one. The seed and fruition are one. Pure essence of mind and luminous mind are one.

Particularly in *Great Garuda* and *Pure Golden Ore*, "pure essence of mind" replaces "luminous mind." "Pure essence of mind" is preferable because it denotes potentiality rather than actuality. Nothing ever comes into existence or ceases to be, and it remains therefore in a state of potential, as in a womb, which is the nature of luminous mind, and is described as "the all-inclusive nucleus" (*thig le chen po*) and "the six nuclei" (*thig le drug*, see note 17). In *Great Garuda* the emergent nature of the pure essence of mind is pure being, "individuated" emptiness (GG2). This essence is our all-inclusive identity, and that is the wish-fulfilling gem (GGc13). It is all-encompassing creativity ("radical creativity") (GG22). In the pure essence of mind, the ultimate samadhi arises as pristine awareness in the field of reality (GG23).

In *Pure Golden Ore* the pure essence of mind is identified with Manjushri Kumara, the all-inclusive buddha-body deity of the eight mahayoga buddhas, who is the fount of all phenomena and thus all experience. All such experience is spontaneously released in the pure-essence-of-mind modality. Thus the pure essence of luminous mind is "the mother of the sugatas" (*sugatagarbha*). In the pure essence of mind, luminous mind and the proclivities of mind are one—there is no separation. The nature of the pure essence of mind is self-sprung awareness, unchanging and imperturbable. It is inconceivable, always present like space, transcending ideas and speech.

In *Eternal Victory Banner* the pure essence of mind is the place of all suffering, where forever comprehended, never becoming anything more or less than luminous mind, it manifests as pure being and pristine awareness (VBc1). All dualities are congruent in the pure essence of mind: therein pure buddha pleasure and the happiness and misery of ordinary beings are one (VBc10). The reality of pleasure and pain, happiness and sadness, and the five passions is identical in the pure essence of mind. Man and woman are identical in the pure essence of mind (VB33). The field of reality in the pure essence of mind remains unmoved by mentation (VB11). Desire, anger, and bewilderment arise in the modality of the pure essence of mind (VBc16). "The essence of luminous mind is the universal source, and the entire reality is pure and simple," at once indeterminate reality itself and the source of reality (VB22).

Pure presence (*rig pa*)

Rig pa is best defined as nondual awareness of our every moment of experience. As the verb "to know" in dualistic verbal structures, it is elevated in Dzogchen jargon to denote the realization of natural perfection. Since we have no equivalent of this notion in the English language, I have used the phrase "pure presence" herein, a phrase that should be taken to imply full awareness of the nondual holistic natural state of being. The word appears only once in the transmissions, where it is used to describe Samantabhadra's pure-pleasure awareness (VB42), and then infrequently in the commentary to *Eternal Victory Banner,* which indicates a late movement to the center of Dzogchen exegesis. Here pure presence is the transcendental realization that subsumes all conceptual meditation (VBc13). It cannot be cultivated, and intrinsic to unstructured reality it is free of dualistic perception; discursive thought arising therein is pristine awareness itself (VBc12). Here pure presence would be represented iconographically as the single naked blue buddha Samantabhadra. But this totality of pure presence is also described as a timeless union of pure presence and basic spaciousness (dharmadhatu), in which pure presence is the skillful means and basic spaciousness the insight function (VBc5). Likewise, whereas basic spaciousness is represented by the vowels of articulated expression, so pure presence is represented by the consonants (VBc18). The union of vowels and consonants is the display of Samantabhadra that never crystalizes. This display of spontaneity is a dance of pure presence (VBc52). In the radical Dzogchen of the transmissions, it is hard to avoid the conclusion that *rig pa* is knowledge of the common light of day.

Reality (*chos nyid, dharmata*)

The Dzogchen reality of luminous mind is nondual reality, and that is all that should be said about it. Insofar as the view and meditation of atiyoga is a constant recognition of deconstructed mind and experience, it provides that reality. Etymologically both the Sanskrit and the Tibetan words mean "experience (dharma) in itself." The word appears only seven times in the transmissions, but although reality is surely their nature and their purpose, it is not exclusive to any particular experience or phenomenon (RC5); it is free and open and all-inclusive (GG18); unsought, it is known in nonmeditation (VB7); it cannot be transmitted through time (VB8); it is adorned by sensual pleasure in basic spaciousness (VB16); it is pure and simple and cannot be elaborated (VB22); and it is noncontingent (VB41).

Reality is inexpressible and the adjectives used to describe it in the *Ten Sutras* all point to that ineffability through negation. It is nondual (CSc), superseding linear time (VB48) and space (VB31), pleasure and pain (VBc15), and the five passions (VBc15); it is not created (CSc and VBc6); it is nondiscursive (GGc1); it cannot be located (GGc3) and it cannot be discovered; it cannot be objectified (GGc1); it is insubstantial (GGc15); it is unelaborated and indeterminable (VBc12); it is immovable (VBc3) and unchangeable (VB41–43); it is signless (VBc21); and it cannot be accomplished or attested (VBc55).

On the other hand, reality is defined positively as Vajrasattva, luminous mind (RCc2 and VBc16), as the here and now ("suchness") (CSc), as pristine awareness (GGc3), as sameness (GGc3), as our dharmakaya identity (VBc3), as one totality (VBc22); its nature is spontaneous pure pleasure (VBc26); it is a display of blissfulness (GGc5); it is the Dzogchen modality itself (VBc21); it is identical to loving-kindness and compassion (VBc2). It is a timeless unchanging moment (VB41–43).

Realization (*rtogs pa*)

The word *rtogs pa*, often translated as "realization" or "intuitive understanding," is linguistically rooted in the verb *rtog pa*, "to think." Mental structure and thought as functions of the rational, intellectual mind are coincident with realization of the nature of mind as empty and radiant (GGc1). The modality of natural perfection is inherent in every thought form. In later Dzogchen exegesis, thought, or the stream of discursive mentation (*rnam rtog*), is conceived of more as a glitch in the luminous-mind modality rather than as a basis for realization. Insofar as we know reality as nothing other than mental constructs, we are never free of "realization." In the transmissions, and particularly in *Eternal Victory Banner* commentary, thought, like passion, is inseparable from luminous mind itself and therefore never to be avoided or suppressed. The seemingly indiscriminate use of *rtog pa* and *rtogs pa* in the texts may be an error of grammar or calligraphy, but their proximate identity is thereby indicated.

Sameness; equality (*mnyam pa*; *mnyam nyid*)

"Sameness" describes the nature of Samantabhadra himself, who is the Lord of Sameness (VB33); "sovereign sameness" is the nature of luminous mind, the luminous-mind matrix, and therefore of all things whatsoever (RC3). This "sameness" is synonymous with "identity" in the sense that the nature of mind is identical in every moment of the here and now. "Sameness" is an attribute of the ocean and also of the sky. Sameness, however, is a state of being, a state of "evenness" or "equanimity," in which there is neither radiation nor absorption. In its imperturbability, it is the antidote to desire and attachment (VBc32). While still imperturbable it is present in the active sphere of Samantabhadra and as such is both the intrinsic identity of multiplicity and multiplicity itself in the same way that reality is both luminous mind matrix and luminous mind manifest. In this way sameness is virtually synonymous with emptiness (*stong pa nyid*) although it has a stronger, positive flavor. It is the nature of pure presence (*rig pa*). It is the unthought dharmakaya. It is reality (*chos nyid*) itself.

"Sameness," in Tibetan, as it does in English, carries the sense of a groundedness and thus is free of all "complacency and arrogance" (VBc14). Sameness, besides taking the sting out of desire and attachment, is the antidote to guilt and remorse. Indeed, as in tantrayoga, sexual indulgence and antisocial activity can be the skillful means of recognition of sameness. It is this fundamental quality of luminous mind that brings the saint and the sinner onto a level playing field.

Union (*sbyor ba*)

The notion of "union," sexual or metaphysical, belongs in the tantric domain. Yet sexual union as the spontaneous play of Samantabhadra's emanation is buddha activity (RC4) and his display itself may be conceived as the union of vowels and consonants (VB18–19). In the commentary on *Eternal Victory Banner*, the union of skillful means and insight is treated under the rubric of anuyoga (VB5). Whereas in tantrayoga the notion of union would be employed as circumlocution to indicate a timeless immanent interfusion (VB34), which may appear as a flash of spontaneous cognition or "non-union" (VB52). In the deconstruction of the tantric ganachakra rite, union is a timeless, endless dance (VBc52).

ༀ

SELECT BIBLIOGRAPHY

Clemente, Adriano. 1999. *The Total Space of Vajrasattva*. Shang Shung Edizioni.

Dowman, Keith. 2003. *The Flight of the Garuda*. Revised edition. Boston: Wisdom Publications.

———. 2009. *Natural Perfection*. Boston: Wisdom Publications.

———. 2010. *Maya-Yoga*. Kathmandu: Vajra Publications.

Dudjom Lingpa. 1994. *Buddhahood without Meditation*. Translated by Richard Barron. Padma Publishing.

Dudjom Rinpoche. 1991. *The Nyingma School of Tibetan Buddhism: Its Fundamentals and History*, 2 vols. Translated by Gyurme Dorje and Matthew Kapstein. Boston: Wisdom Publications.

Germano, David. 1992. "Poetic Thought, the Intelligent Universe, and the Mystery of Self: The Tantric Synthesis of Dzogchen in Fourteenth Century Tibet." Unpublished doctoral dissertation.

———. 2005. "The Funerary Transformation of the Great Perfection." *Journal of the International Association of Tibetan Studies* 1 (October): 1–54.

Guenther, Herbert. 1984. *Matrix of Mystery*. Boston: Shambhala.

Karmay, Samten. 2007. *The Great Perfection*. Leiden, Netherlands: Brill.

Longchenpa. 1987. *You Are the Eyes of the World*. Translated by Kennard Lipman and Merrill Peterson with Namkhai Norbu. Novato, CA: Lotsawa Publications.

Low, James. 1998. *Simply Being*. London: Vajra Press.

Norbu, Namkhai, and John Shane. 1986. *The Crystal and the Way of Light*. London: RKP.

Norbu, Namkhai, and Kennard Lipman. 1987. *Primordial Experience*. Boston: Shambhala.

Norbu, Namkhai, and Adriano Clemente. 1989. *Dzogchen: The Self-Perfected State*. London: Arkana.

———. 1999. *The Supreme Source: The Fundamental Tantra of the Dzogchen Semde*. Ithaca, NY: Snow Lion Publications.

Nyoshul Khenpo. 1995. *Natural Great Perfection*. Translated by Surya Das. Ithaca, NY: Snow Lion Publications.

Reynolds, John M. 1996. *Golden Letters*. Ithaca, NY: Snow Lion Publications.

Thondup, Tulku. 1989. *Buddha Mind: An Anthology of Longchen Rabjampa's Writing on Dzogpa Chenpo*. Ithaca, NY: Snow Lion Publications.

Valby, Jim, trans. 2011. *Ornament of the State of Samantabhadra*, 3 vols. Shelburne Falls, MA: Jim Valby Publications.

Yudra Nyingpo. 2004. *The Great Image: The Life Story of Vairochana, the Translator*. Translated by Ani Jinba Palmo. Boston: Shambhala.

Index

About the Translator

A CULTURAL REFUGEE from his native England, Keith Dowman arrived in Benares, India, in 1966, having travelled overland from Europe. Apart from an occasional foray back to the West he has spent a lifetime in India and Nepal, not always in Tibetan refugee society, engaged in existential Buddhadharma. He has lived as a yogin, monk, pilgrim, and then as a householder, and as a scholar and poet free from any institutional constriction.

In India in the '60s he was fortunate enough to encounter the grandfather-lama refugees arriving in India in the wake of the Chinese invasion of Tibet. In those heady years when the old lamas were totally receptive to the solicitation of Western disciples seeking confirmation of the validity of their existential trajectories, he received initiation, empowerment, pith instruction, and personal guidance from Dudjom Rimpoche Jigdral Yeshe Dorje and Kanjur Rimpoche Longchen Yeshe Dorje, who became his root gurus, among many other Nyingma lamas and lamas of other schools, notably the Eighth Khamtrul Rimpoche and the Sixteenth Karmapa Rikpai Dorje. As Chogyal Namkhai Norbu remarked, "In communion with many great masters [Keith Dowman] has fortuitously absorbed the realization of Dzogchen."

In the '80s he translated various Vajrayana texts and when Tibet opened three years of seasonal trekking in central Tibet resulted in a pilgrims' guide to Tibet. More recently, he has concentrated exclusively on the translation of Dzogchen texts. Likewise, although he has taught Vajrayana since 1992, more recently he has focused entirely on Dzogchen. He lives a peripatetic lifestyle teaching the radical Dzogchen derived from the early Nyingma tantras that is free of the tendency toward the spiritual materialism so evident in Western Buddhism, a dharma easily assimilable into Western culture.

OTHER TITLES BY KEITH DOWMAN

Spaciousness: Longchenpa's Treasury of the Dharmadhatu (forthcoming)

The Great Secret of Mind (trans.)

Maya-Yoga

Natural Perfection (Old Man Basking in the Sun)

The Flight of the Garuda

The Sacred Life of Tibet

Power-Places of Kathmandu

Boudhanath: The Great Stupa

Masters of Enchantment

The Power-Places of Central Tibet: The Pilgrims Guide

Masters of Mahamudra

Sky Dancer: The Secret Life and Songs of the Lady Yeshe Tsogyel

The Nyingma Icons

The Divine Madman: The Life and Songs of Drukpa Kunley

The Legend of the Great Stupa

Calm and Clear: A Manual of Buddhist Meditation

About Wisdom Publications

WISDOM PUBLICATIONS is dedicated to offering works relating to and inspired by Buddhist traditions.

To learn more about us or to explore our other books, please visit our website at www.wisdompubs.org.

You can subscribe to our e-newsletter or request our print catalog online, or by writing to:

Wisdom Publications
199 Elm Street
Somerville, Massachusetts 02144 USA

You can also contact us at 617-776-7416, or info@wisdompubs.org.

Wisdom is a nonprofit, charitable 501(c)(3) organization, and donations in support of our mission are tax deductible.

Wisdom Publications is affiliated with the Foundation for the Preservation of the Mahayana Tradition (FPMT).